Independent Living for the Handicapped and the Elderly

Independent Living for the Handicapped and the Elderly

Elizabeth Eckhardt May
Former Dean, School of Home Economics, University of Connecticut

Neva R. Waggoner
Consultant, Rehabilitation in Homemaking

Eleanor Boettke Hotte
Professor, Clothing and Textiles, School of Home Economics, University of Connecticut

Houghton Mifflin Company   Boston
Atlanta   Dallas   Geneva, Illinois   Hopewell, New Jersey   Palo Alto   London

Photographs by Jerauld A. Manter and from International Sources

Library of Congress Catalog Card Number: 73–11770
ISBN 0–395–18108–9

Contents

Preface

This is a "Here's How" book for the men, women, and children with physical limitations who would like to live as independently as possible—for as long as possible. It is also designed for their families and for students and professional personnel in the fields of rehabilitation, home management, housing, clothing, child development, and family relations.

Inspired by the late Lillian M. Gilbreth, world famous industrial engineer, the book demonstrates ways in which the work simplification principles used by management experts in industry may be applied to the home and thus enable handicapped or elderly persons to live more independently.

The problem of dressing, an important part of independent living, is covered in three chapters devoted to the design and adaptation of clothing. The emphasis is on clothing that is becoming, comfortable, easy to handle, and an aid in disguising disabilities.

Another section is devoted to work simplification principles as applied to the care of young children by parents or grandparents who have physical limitations. There is also a section devoted to play and recreational activities that adults may share with children, resulting in cooperative behavior and warm companionship.

Although the focus of this book is primarily on those with orthopedic difficulties or with low energy, much of it can be valuable to persons with other limitations, and in fact, to those with no limitations at all. The material represents studies of nearly 300 programs on independent living in the United States and Canada, and in ten foreign countries.

Based on its now out-of-print predecessor, *Homemaking for the Handicapped*, by the same authors, this is now the only hardbound book of its kind in the field. The authors are indebted to many people who had a part in the research on which this book is based. Among them are our consultants, Dr. Lillian M. Gilbreth, industrial engineer; Dr. Charles O. Bechtol, orthopedic surgeon; Julia Judson, physical therapist and home management specialist, and the members of the research staff in the School of Home Economics at the University of Connecticut who made major contributions: Dr. Jessie S. Wall, child development; Mrs. Gertrude M. Zmola and Mrs. Sylvia Aho, home management, and Mrs. Alice P. Whitaker, clothing and visual aids. It is a tribute to their pioneering efforts that much of the material they helped to develop will continue to be useful.

THE AUTHORS

Independent Living for the Handicapped and the Elderly

Housekeeping from a wheelchair can be done with ease when working surfaces are high enough to permit knee room and when equipment is placed "within easy reach" and "in the place of first use."

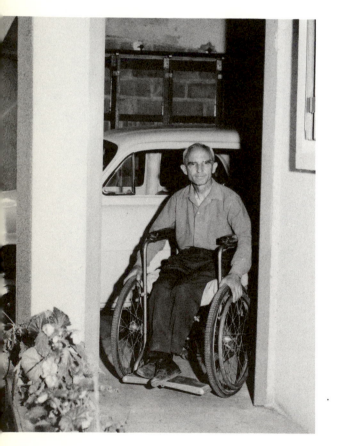

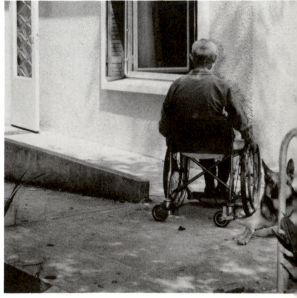

Ramps lead from the door to the garage and to the street. This man loves gardening and has a flower box set up at the end of his parallel bars in the yard. He leans on the bars and does his "standing exercises" while he does his gardening.

CHAPTER 1

Where There's
A Will

It takes only two letters to change the word *dependent* into the word *independent*, but for the person with low energy or other physical limitations these two letters may have a lifetime of significance. It is not the nature of the disability that necessarily determines where a handicapped or an elderly person will live but rather the degree of his dependence or independence in managing the everyday essential tasks related to food, shelter, and clothing. The alternatives are few; unless he learns to carry on the necessary household tasks himself, he must have someone else do them for him, or he must live in an institution that provides physical care.

For many persons with physical limitations the task of developing even a small degree of independence in performing household tasks may seem overwhelming. Achievement requires the simplification of the work to be done, the support of the medical team, the cooperation of the family and the community, and for the person concerned, an enormous amount of courage and determination!

The maintenance of even a simple home involves a multitude of details. Someone must plan the meals, purchase the food, prepare and serve the meals, and wash and store the dishes. Someone must make the beds and keep the house clean and in good repair. Someone must select and purchase the clothing for the family and be responsible for keeping it clean and mended, and for families with children, there is a multitude of additional tasks. This book is focused on the simplification of homemaking tasks of five groups of people for whom the prospect of more independent living is a fundamental personal concern: homemakers with physical limitations, men and women in the "older age group," accident victims, handicapped children, and disabled veterans.

The Homemaker with Physical Limitations

Consider first the problems of the mother who is handicapped through accident or disease; since she is unable to choose some other vocation that would take her physical limitations into account, she must go back to her old job and manage it, somehow! Unless some of her work is simplified or shared or eliminated, there is little energy left for her more important responsibility of being a good wife and mother.

With a well-constructed ramp, mother can come too! When the neighbors' children come into her yard for a ball game she is their favorite umpire.

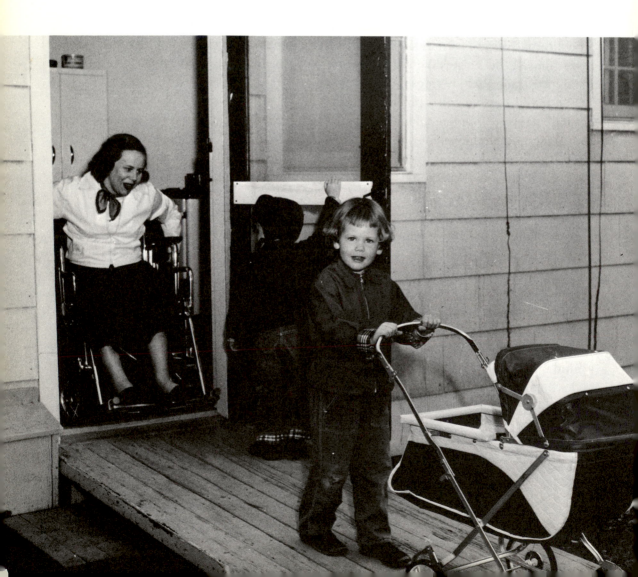

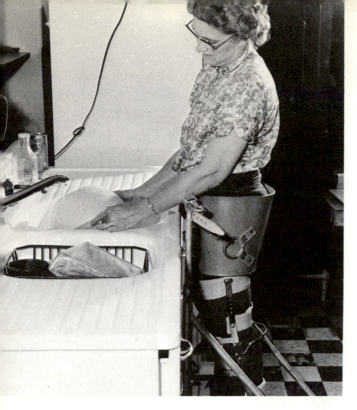

In a plea for including handicapped homemakers as "workers" and there-fore making them eligible to share in federal and state vocational rehabilita-tion programs, the late Mary E. Switzer, H.E.W. Commissioner of Social and Rehabilitation Services, gave her opinion on the importance of this part of the rehabilitation program:

> There are nearly 40 million women "keeping house" in the United States. The multiplicity of skills they must possess and the hours they must work are matched by few requirements for jobs held by men. If an arbitrary value were placed upon the homemaker's services, and she was paid accordingly, her annual wage would be, to say the least, substantial. Thus, when a housewife is unable to perform her duties, an economic benefit to the nation is lost. Far worse, the family upon which she has focused all her efforts will suffer or even disintegrate.
>
> Among those women whose usual activity is keeping house there are 4,600,000 or nearly 12 per cent, who are victims of such disabilities as faulty vision, arthritis, paralysis, or circulatory disease. These handicaps, in one manner or another, limit them in the performance of household tasks.[1]

[1] Elizabeth E. May, Neva R. Waggoner, and Eleanor M. Botteke, *Homemaking for the Handicapped,* (New York: Dodd, Mead and Company, 1966), p. xiii.

The importance of a well organized household to the mental and physical health of the family is pointed up by Dr. Bernice Moore of the Hogg Foundation:

> In no facet of living is disorganization more tension giving, than in home and family life. Tensions are contagious. Having available what family members need, when they need it, cannot be understated in terms of economic worth nor in terms of emotional stability.[2]

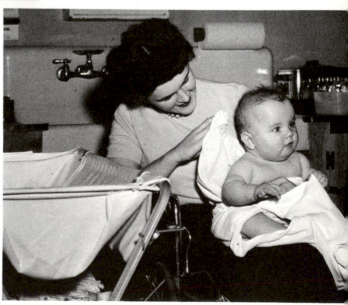

[2] Beatrice Moore, "Time, Tension and Mental Health," *Journal of Home Economics*, January 1957, p. 17.

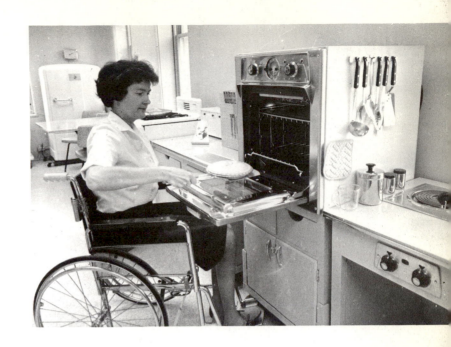

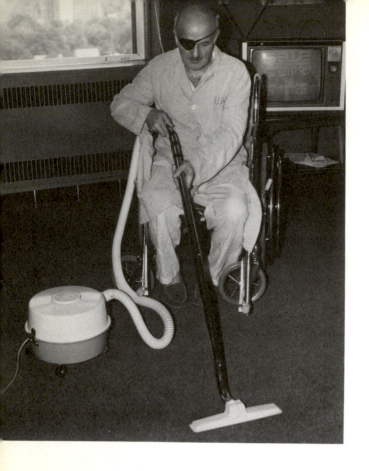

Independent living for as long as possible. . . .

The Older Age Group

The fact that they are classified together in the census report is one of the few things men and women who are "65 or over" have in common. Even though the age range is from 65 to 125, society continues to lump them all together as "senior citizens"![3] This goes on regardless of tremendous differences in physical fitness, educational background, work experience, achievements, financial reserves, personal philosophy or purpose in life. But in spite of their many differences *all older people must sooner or later face the same question: how long will they be able to go on living independently?*

[3] In 1971 Social Security paid benefits to 5,200 people 100 years old or older. U.S. Administration on Aging, H.E.W. *Facts and Figures on Older Americans, An Overview 1971*, #5 D.H.E.W. Publication #(S.R.S.) 73–20005. First Printing 1972, p. 2.

The number of older people who are concerned over where they will live and who will take care of them when they are no longer able to care for themselves is increasing every day. In 1900 they numbered 1 out of 25 persons in the population. In 1970 they numbered nearly 1 out of 10.

CHANGE IN PERCENTAGE OF OLDER PEOPLE IN POPULATION

CENSUS FIGURES	POPULATION	65 OR OVER	APPROXIMATE NO. IN POPULATION
1900	76,000,000	3,100,000	1 out of every 25
*1950	151,300,000	12,300,000	1 out of every 8
*1960	179,300,000	16,600,000	1 out of every 9
*1970	203,165,699	20,049,592	1 out of every 10

*Includes Alaska and Hawaii.

U.S. Administration on Aging, *Facts and Figures on Older Americans, An Overview 1971.* #5 D.H.E.W. Publication #(S.R.S.) 73–20005. 1972, p. 2.

Another significant change is in the increase in the number of women compared to the number of men. In 1900 the number of men and the number of women in the older age group was about equal, but in 1970 there were 139 women per 100 men in the age group 65 or over and among those 75 or over, there were 156 women per 100 men.[4]

For many older men and women, the question of independent living versus some kind of institutional care is a matter of great personal concern. The 1970 census reported that in every 100 older persons, 18% of the men and 54.6% of the women are widowed. In every 100, 7 men and 21 women live alone or with non-relatives. Approximately, 1,000,000, or *one out of 20*, lived in institutions.[4]

There are few older people who would not choose to maintain their independence for as long as possible, and for many the dearest wish may be to continue to live in their own homes. To do this they must face the fact that there will be an inevitable decline in both energy and mobility that may eventually require a new pattern of living.

[4] *Ibid.*, p. 7.

In the year 2000, if the prediction holds, there will be 28,000,000 older Americans.[5] *The simplification of their lifestyle,* preferably before it is necessary, could be a large factor in helping them to maintain a maximum degree of independence for as long as possible.

Accident Victims

For the millions of people who suffer either temporary or permanent disability because of an accident, the question of dependence versus independence suddenly becomes a very personal matter. This was true for the 11,200,000 men, women, and children accident victims reported by the National Safety Council in 1971. Motor vehicle accidents were responsible for 2,000,000 of these injuries, but 4,200,000 occurred in the home; falls head the list of causes of injury and burns come second.[6, 7]

Handicapped Children

Future living arrangements for handicapped children are easy to predict. Unless they can gradually learn to look after themselves, it will be necessary for someone else to take care of their everyday needs for the rest of their lives. But far more important than the saving of the time of the parent or nurse is the fact that by becoming more independent, a child may develop greater self-confidence and initiative. This will carry over into all of his activities. For him this may lead to a lifetime of independent living rather than a lifetime of institutional care after his parents are gone.

[5] *Ibid.,* p. 7.

[6] 1972 Accidental Death Report for 1971—total accidental deaths: 115,000; from motor vehicles: 54,000; accidents in the home: 27,500. National Safety Council, *Accident Facts, 1972 Edition,* p. 3.

[7] In addition to the nearly 2,000,000 killed in automobile accidents in the past 50 years, an additional 106,342,000 have been maimed or seriously injured. *World Magazine,* March 13, 1973, Editor's Notes.

The number of handicapped children in our country is unbelievably large! Birth defects alone account for some type of disability in one baby in every fourteen[8] and over 1,000,000 children under age 17 have some type of physical or mental handicap.[9]

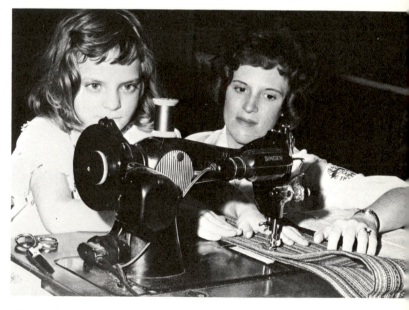

[8] National Foundation—March of Dimes, *Facts, 1973*, p. 8.
[9] U.S. Dept. of Health, Education and Welfare, *National Health Statistics Report, 1970*, Series 10, Number 72, Table 9, p. 15.

Early training may lead to a lifetime of independent living.

A child who was a "thalidomide baby" gains a degree of independence and an enormous sense of achievement in making cupcakes.

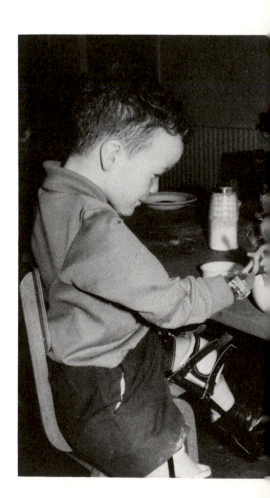

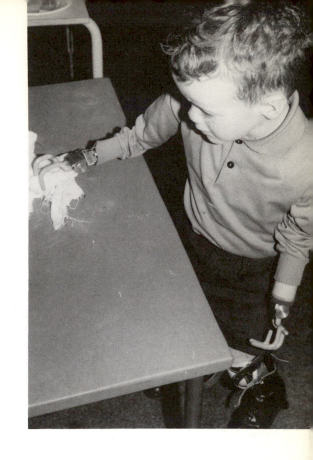

Disabled Veterans

Something new is being included in rehabilitation programs in veterans' hospitals. In some, there are small apartments complete with kitchens, "where a guy can learn to shift for himself." Those who can become even partially independent are the ones likely to be "discharged" to return to their families or to some other plan for living outside hospital walls. Even though the families of disabled veterans may be devoted and concerned, few are able to care for persons who are totally dependent for 24 hours of the day.

The 1970 census reported some pertinent figures concerning the 28,112,495 veterans of all wars, beginning with World War I.[10] Of this group nearly 500,000 receive some type of prosthetic aid.[11]

If you can't fix lunch for yourself, you will just have to depend on someone else to fix it for you.

[10] 1970 Census, news release, April 25, 1973. C–B73–104.
[11] Charles J. Ashley, Veterans Administration memorandum, April 11, 1973. Total number receiving "prosthetic aid" was 497,119. (World War I: 9,187; World War II: 299,653; Korea: 46,371; Vietnam: 51,404.)

In spite of his weak arms and limited grasp, this young man, a quadriplegic, can use portable cooking equipment when it is placed at the right height.

Another grim report concerns veterans living in institutions. In 1970 nearly 300,000 were reported living in hospitals for mental, tubercular, and chronic diseases, in nursing homes and homes for the aged and dependent, and in other institutions.[12] The alternatives for veterans are the same as they are for any other group of handicapped persons. As one expressed it: "If a guy can't fry an egg for himself someone else will have to fry it for him!"

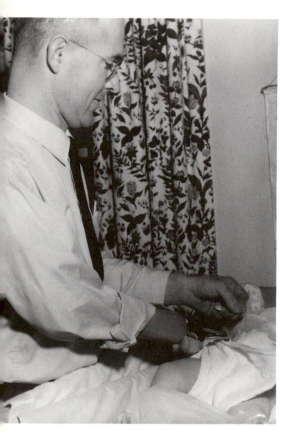

When a small daughter needs help, there is a lot of satisfaction in knowing you can manage the safety pins for an important garment.

[12] 1970 Census, U.S. Bureau of the Census, "Characteristics of Civilian Male Veterans," P.C. (S1)–33 Supplementary Report, March 1973. Total number of inmates of institutions was 287,183 (16–49 years old: 157,253; 50–64 years old: 54,664; 65–74 years old: 40,748; 75 or over: 34,518).

Lillian M. Gilbreth (1878–1972)

Dr. Gilbreth is internationally known as an industrial engineer and a pioneer in work simplification. She is also the mother of a large family made famous by the book and motion picture "Cheaper by the Dozen," written by two of her children. Her lifetime concern was to save precious human energy and time for all workers but especially for those with physical limitations. Her motto "Where There's a Will—There's a Way" is the theme of this book.

CHAPTER 2

Management Principles Demonstrated by Homemakers with Physical Limitations

Many homemakers have learned better methods for managing their households from the motion and time study research done nearly fifty years ago by two industrial engineers, Frank and Lillian Gilbreth. They pioneered in developing a scientific approach to the study of ways in which industrial workers might improve their work methods and save energy and time. The principles of work simplification which they developed have since been applied to the problems of workers in libraries, in hospitals, on farms, and in this chapter, to the home.

A. The "Questioning Approach"

The first step in the study of work simplification is to ask these six questions:

What is the job to be done?

Why should the job be done; is it necessary?

Where should it be done? Could energy or time be saved if it were done somewhere else?

When should it be done?

Who should do the job? Is this the best investment of the homemaker's energy and time? Could another member of the family do it? Could the family afford to have someone else do it in the home or outside?

How should it be done? Must there be some adaptation of household equipment? Is there need for new tools or appliances? Will the family accept a finished product that takes less work?

The "Questioning Approach" Applied to Dishwashing

After listing all of the tasks to be done in a single day, this homemaker selected *dishwashing* as the first to be analyzed. When broken down into steps, it involves clearing the table, scraping, stacking, washing, rinsing, drying, and storing dishes.

Her standard of housekeeping, before she was limited to the use of one hand, was to dry all of her dishes and store them in a closed cupboard after every single meal so that her kitchen would always appear neat and tidy. This task became awkward and time-consuming.

After using the "questioning approach" in analyzing the task of dishwashing, this homemaker has eliminated a time-consuming part of the job—the drying of the dishes one by one and putting them away. She now scalds her dishes and leaves them to air-dry, thus saving nearly an hour every day.

The "Questioning Approach" Applied to a Laundry Problem

Since she must now contend with poor balance and difficulty in walking, this homemaker finds it burdensome to drag the basket of heavy, wet clothes to the outdoor line.

After subjecting her laundry problem to the "questioning approach," this homemaker used a cart on wheels, instead of a laundry basket, and arranged for a pulley clothesline, set at a good working height, on her porch outside of the kitchen.

She is still considering other aspects of her problem of laundry management. Should she send at least some of it to a commercial laundry? Should she invest her time in other tasks and delegate this one to some other member of the family? Should she buy a dryer and thus eliminate the task of hanging out clothes? Should she try to cut down on the amount of laundry by using plastic mats and paper napkins more often? Should she select more drip-dry clothes that require little ironing?

B. Principles of Work Simplification
Demonstrated by Homemakers with Physical Limitations

Some of the new work methods developed by homemakers with physical limitations are based on Dr. Gilbreth's principles of work simplification listed in "Management in the Home" (I-55).

1. *Arrange a Special Work Place for Each Job*

Adjust work place height to the woman and the job, to encourage good posture and diminish fatigue. Different jobs will require different heights.

Lay out work areas within normal reach. Work where areas for both hands overlap, and arrange supplies in semicircle within easy reach.

Have fixed work places: a special place to do each job, so that supplies and equipment may be stored there ready for use.

Pre-position tools and supplies. Store small tools so that they can be grasped and used immediately. Hang measuring cups and spoons separately within view.

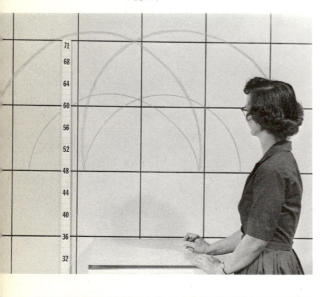

Arrange for best working conditions— good light, ventilation, pleasing colors, order, comfortable clothing.

A. ADJUST THE WORK PLACE HEIGHT TO THE WOMAN AND THE JOB

Since the reach arc varies greatly for a non-handicapped homemaker, a homemaker limited to the use of her right arm, and a homemaker confined to a wheelchair, their working heights must be adjusted accordingly.

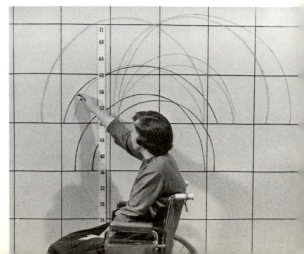

B. HAVE A SPECIAL PLACE TO DO EACH JOB

This laundry area, designed for a homemaker limited to the use of her right arm, shows the importance of adjusting storage and arranging equipment to suit her range of motion. The washer and dryer are placed so she can work to the front and to her right with a minimum of cross-backs to the left. This gives an easy flow to her work.

This laundry area is organized so that there is an "easy flow of work." An adjustable ironing board, an ironer, and a sorting table are all within easy reach. She has a carton for each member of the family into which she sorts the clothing as it is folded.

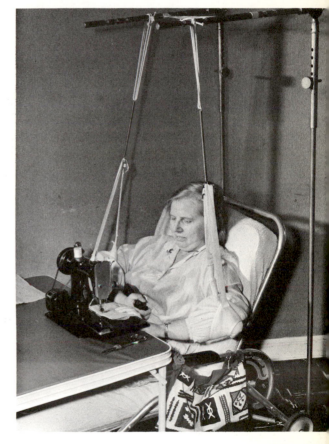

A card table with legs lengthened proved to be just the right working height for this homemaker. She is learning to manage the foot control with her hand. Supplies are easy to reach. She is looking forward to making a dress for her daughter. This is the first time during her long illness that she has been able to do something for someone else.

2. *Select the Right Tools and Equipment to Do the Job*

Reduce activity to fewest elements. Select equipment that can be used for more than one job. Eliminate unnecessary motions like "smoothing" a bed.

Locate machine switches and controls within easy reach. Select appliances with accessible controls. Change location of switches where possible, or use electric cords with their own switches.

Select tools suited to the job and to the person doing the job. (For example, longer handles to extend reach.)

When work centers are too high and allow no knee room, the problem of reaching controls is difficult and sometimes impossible.

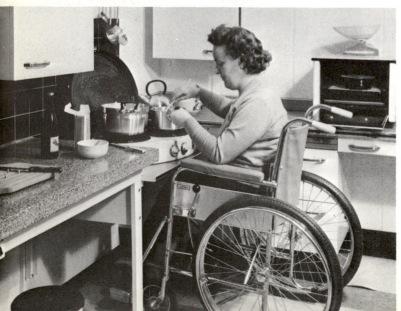

When controls are located on front side of the stove, they are easy to manage from a wheelchair. Note the comfortable work height and the knee room of this food preparation unit. The counter, the stove, and the oven are on the same level, which makes it possible to slide utensils instead of lifting them.

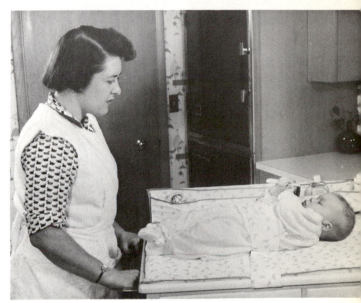

3. *Choose Equipment for Multiple Use*

Dressing cart provides convenient storage for all items needed in bathing
   and dressing as well as a safe place for dressing the baby.

The drawer pulls are large and easy to grasp.

Drawers have nylon glides and are easy to open and close.

Safety strap has Velcro closure.

Heavy towel bars at the end provide a sturdy support for the mother with
   poor balance who has difficulty in walking and standing.

Since the mother also has difficulty in lifting and carrying, the cart provides
   a safe, easy way to transport baby (A).

4. Use the Body Efficently

Sit to work when possible unless standing is part of the therapy. The chair should be comfortable—not just any chair. There should be adequate support for the back but the shoulders should be free to turn. Feet should rest flat on the floor. A stool is useful for short time jobs; the height to be determined by the particular needs of the individual.

Slide things instead of lifting and carrying. Slide pots from range to counter. (This necessitates uniform heights.) Use cart or wheel table or basket whenever possible instead of carrying laundry, groceries, dishes, etc. A table on wheels, the same height as the open oven door, can be used with ease and safety in transferring hot dishes. This is especially true when the oven is set at counter height. If possible put good casters on everything that must be moved such as kitchen tables or ironing boards or a dolly for moving pails. If the storage area is on the same level as the floor the amount of lifting necessary can be greatly reduced.

Use gravity and momentum wherever possible: laundry chute, gravity feed bins, pan below level of cutting board. Use weight of sheets and blankets to assist in folding and unfolding.

Use both hands in opposite and symmetrical ways if possible. Use smooth flowing motions in curved path rather than short jerky angular ones. This plan works well for such tasks as dusting and polishing. Avoid having one hand lie idle while the other does most of the work; many tasks can be done twice as fast if both hands are used. This is especially true of such tasks as taking eggs from a carton, setting a table, washing and storing dishes, bed making, etc.

Avoid holding. Use flat bottomed utensils that rest firmly on the stove; these are safer and more efficient. Use suction cups, clamps, cleats, or other holding devices so that both hands are free to work. (This is of special importance to the person limited to the use of one hand.) A pull-out board, set at a comfortable height, may have a hole for stabilizing bowls. "Collars" of different sizes may be inserted to accommodate bowls of different sizes.

Use other parts of body when possible in order to free the hands. This will vary with each individual. Sometimes jars may be held firmly between the knees; in folding a towel the corner may be held between the teeth to free the hands; some items can be held by the feet to keep hands free.

Use lowest class motions. (The use of fingers alone would be considered the "lowest class motion." The next step would be fingers and wrist and progressively: the forearm, the upper arm and finally the whole body. For example: Pressing a button to start an electric mixer takes a lot less energy than using an egg beater or a mixing spoon.)

A. SIT TO WORK WHEN ADVISABLE

Sit to work cannot be an absolute rule. It may be that standing is part of the prescribed therapy program for the handicapped person. Then, too, standing may take less energy than getting up and down frequently for short-time jobs.

For long tasks, a pleasant, comfortable place to sit is desirable. Well-chosen tools include a sharp knife and a cutting board.

B. SLIDE THINGS INSTEAD OF LIFTING

Casters on the bottoms of stools or ironing boards help in transporting them without lifting.

C. USE OTHER PARTS OF THE BODY TO TAKE THE PLACE OF A MISSING MEMBER

By holding the attachment between her knees, this homemaker can manage the task of keeping the house clean. The vacuum cleaner is on wheels and can be moved easily with her foot.

D. USE MECHANICAL DEVICES FOR HOLDING

Those limited to the use of one hand are forced to stabilize equipment. This young woman has just been introduced to a simple device for stabilizing an egg beater. Stabilization of equipment is also a good idea for persons with full use of both hands. Too often the use of one hand is wasted in holding something which could be held mechanically.

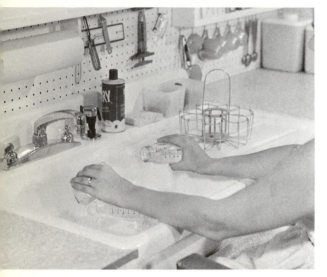

E. USE BOTH HANDS WHEN POSSIBLE

By the rhythmic use of both hands this mother is able to rinse bottles in half the time it takes her to rinse them with one hand. Working with two hands is also helpful in such jobs as removing eggs from a carton, using two dust mitts instead of one, and reaching for two dishes at one time when clearing the table or putting dishes in the cupboard.

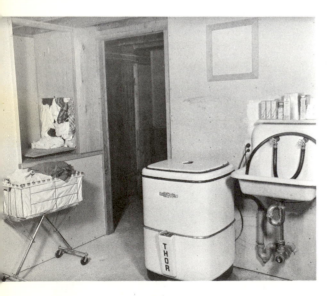

F. MAKE USE OF GRAVITY AND MOMENTUM

It is not necessary for anyone in this family to carry the soiled clothes downstairs. They are dropped into the clothes chute in the bathroom and slide to the basement laundry. They are sorted on the counter where they fall.

CHAPTER 3

Work Simplification Principles Applied to Household Tasks: Laundry and Formula Making

Good laundry management, equipment, tools, and procedures simplify home laundry for any homemaker. With hand limitations it may be necessary to develop a new laundry procedure and select tools and equipment that will compensate for the homemaker's particular kind and degree of limitation. After experimenting with different ways of doing the job, each homemaker should be able to work out the best method for her own use.

General Suggestions for Doing the Laundry More Easily

SELECT EQUIPMENT CAREFULLY.

Automatic washers and dryers eliminate much handling of clothes.

Machines must be selected with openings and controls that the homemaker can reach and operate easily.

Lightweight one-handled baskets or laundry carts with large swivel casters help in moving clothes to washer, dryer, or lines.

LOCATE LAUNDRY EQUIPMENT (washers, dryers, lines) *in a convenient place.*

To avoid extra walking, climbing, and reaching store laundry supplies at the laundry center.

CHOOSE.

Fabric and garment designs that are completely machine washable and machine dryable; detergents and cleaning aids that are most effective in the water available and that are packaged in containers that can be opened easily.

PLAN.

Frequent washdays to avoid great piles of laundry that overwork the equipment and the homemaker. (Oversoiled clothes are difficult to wash clean.) Plan for family help for the parts of home laundry that are difficult or impossible to do.

Work Simplification Principles Demonstrated by a Homemaker Limited to the Use of One Hand in Doing the Family Laundry

(1) Soiled clothes are brought to the laundry center in a laundry cart which rolls easily on large swivel wheels.

(2) The diaper load is kept separate by putting wet diapers into a soak solution in a lightweight plastic pail. They are then dropped directly into the automatic washer. The machine does the hard work of rinsing and wringing.

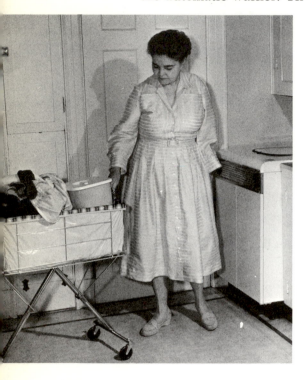

By hand-controlling the washer cycle, the diapers are spun free of soak solution and pre-rinsed in clear water before the complete wash-rinse cycle is started. On this machine, controls are out front—easy to reach and see.

(3) At the beginning of the wash cycle she adds a measured amount of detergent to the diaper load. The machine is then allowed to complete the cycle. The amount of detergent is determined by the water condition, amount of water used in the machine, and the degree of soil of the load being washed.

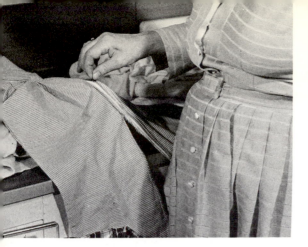

(4) While the diapers wash, she prepares and sorts additional washer loads. In order to close the zipper on a garment she holds it firmly against the counter top with her hip. She finds a 36-inch-high counter a comfortable working height for her. She is careful not to overload the washer, since the results are better if laundry is sorted carefully into small loads according to color, fabric and degree of soil. Fabrics that need special care are set aside for hand washing. To pre-treat spots for either machine or hand laundry, she brushes them with extra detergent. The rubberized grooved drainboard gives her a rough base for scrubbing badly soiled spots.

(5) The rubber plunger (G-33) makes washing easier, since it uses arm muscles instead of fingers as it pulls water and detergent through the fabric to remove soil.

(6) She has learned to wring clothes with only one hand by twisting the garment around the faucet. Since these red socks "bleed" color, they are washed and rinsed by hand. She extracts water from knitted garments by rolling them in a turkish towel.

31

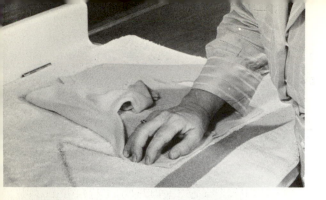

(7) Before washing this sweater, she laid it flat on a towel and drew a line around it with a soft lead pencil. After washing, she laid it on the towel, pulled it into its original shape, and allowed it to dry.

(8) She tries to choose fabrics that will need no ironing but may be straightened on hangers and drip-dried. The hanger can be inserted more easily while the garment is still floating in the rinse water.

(9) The pulley clothesline is attached to the back porch. The height is convenient for her. The clothespin bag is within easy reach. A magnet on the cover keeps it open. The basket with a single handle makes it easy to carry wet clothes from the washer just inside the door. The broad rail is a good support.

Through long practice this homemaker has developed the finger skill necessary for hanging clothes. All of her fingers work to do the job. The ring and little finger hold the garment on the line while the other three fingers hold the pin and push it over the line.

(10) She uses her kitchen counter to hold garments to be folded. The weight of some garments pulls them into natural folds. She holds lightweight items in her teeth to assist in folding. A one-handled basket is used to transport clothes to points of storage.

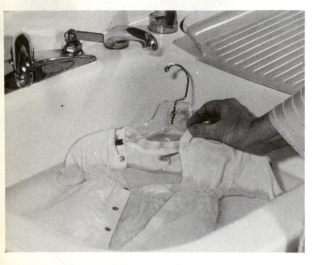

Work Simplification Principles
Applied to the Job of Preparing Baby's Formula
Demonstrated by a Mother Confined to a Wheelchair

Step One: Study the Job to Be Done

Since her baby requires a special formula, she must mix it herself.

Step Two: Selection and Arrangement of Equipment

This kitchen was altered to provide:

Knee room under the mix center and sink center so that the homemaker can work in a forward position.

Counter tops at 30 inches high to allow her to work with upper arms near her sides and her elbows at about a right angle.

A wastebasket, lined with a disposable bag, is located under the sink.

Upper Cupboard Storage, 44 inches high. The lower shelf is a very comfortable reach and with a little stretching she can reach all the storage. The pan file has utensils stored individually so each one can be grasped with a single motion.

By using paper towels she cuts down on washing, ironing, and storage.

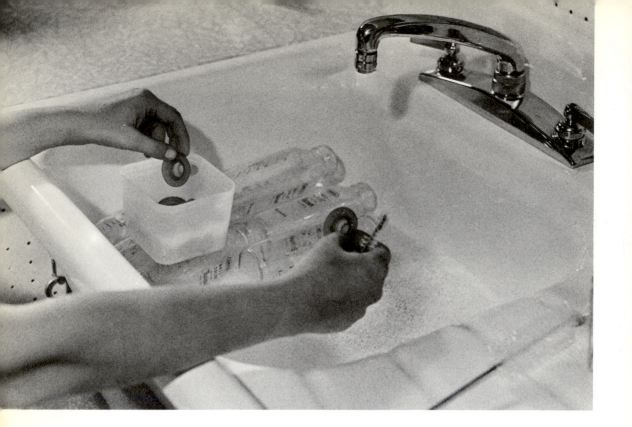

Step Three: Procedure

After each feeding on the previous day, she rinsed the formula bottles, filled them with water, and stored them in the rack in the sterilizer.

A. Before beginning to prepare the formula for the next twenty-four hours, she considered her work sequence. This helped her to avoid delays. First on the list was the task of washing the bottles in the sterilizer.

By using both hands to empty water from bottles, two at a time, she cuts the time for this part of the task in half. The sterilizer rack holds the bottles securely in one unit.

She has put the sterilizer on the stove so the water may start heating and be ready for the sterilizing process after the bottles have been filled with formula. (Bottles, nipples, and formula are all sterilized at the same time.)

B. She puts both hands to work again for the task of washing nipples. The left hand places the washed nipples in the box as the right hand picks up and positions the next nipple for washing. She holds the brush ready for work to avoid searching and picking it up after washing each nipple.

C. A punch opener designed for milk cans is used to make two holes in the can in one operation.

Water for the formula was measured in the graduated pitcher while she was at the sink. The sugar or carbohydrate additive has been measured and added to the warm water so it will start to dissolve.

Her recipe is proportioned to use the entire 13-ounce can of milk so she has no storage of partial cans of milk. This eliminates the use of an extra measuring utensil.

D. By using wide-mouthed bottles and a pitcher, she needs no funnel to fill the bottles. She placed the clean bottles in the rack with the graduate marks facing her so she can easily fill them with the correct amount and transfer them to the sterilizer.

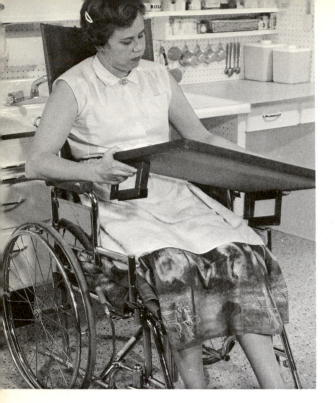

E. After the sterilization period is over and the kettle has cooled, the bottles are removed. This is her most difficult operation, since the stove is a standard 36-inch height that could not be lowered to the 30-inch comfortable counter height.

F. To transport things and to provide a very convenient work surface, she likes this easy-to-attach wheelchair tray which was made to fit her chair.

G. She sets the bottles in a pan for storage in the refrigerator. The tray makes a convenient work surface, since she expects to use it also for transportation of the bottles to the refrigerator.

CHAPTER 4

Work Simplification in the Physical Care of Children

Many physically handicapped young women have proved that a disability is not necessarily a barrier to childbearing.[1]

The decision on whether or not to have a child should not be made by anxious relatives, but rather by the family doctor and the two people chiefly concerned.

Another decision to be made by the parents is whether or not the mother will take over the care of her children, as far as her physical limitations will permit. This is her right and privilege, but if she undertakes this task, it may then be necessary for other members of the family to take over some of the routine housekeeping chores. Decisions must be made concerning which tasks the mother will do, which will be done by someone else, and, also, which are unnecessary and therefore can be eliminated.

[1] A Connecticut study of 100 orthopedically handicapped young mothers showed that 107 of their 225 children were born after the disability occurred.

When a mother chooses to take care of her baby, it is important for her to begin as early as possible to have some part in his care. Young babies are amazingly adaptable and cooperative. An infant will learn to cooperate by holding on if he feels insecure, by raising his body for diapering, or by leaning against his mother as she carries him in her lap in the wheelchair.

Mastering routine tasks will not only give the mother confidence and competence that will carry over into other tasks, but will also help in the development of basic trust and cooperation between the mother and child.

Although these suggestions are intended primarily for mothers with physical limitations, they apply to fathers, too!

Guides for the Selection of Child Care Equipment

The determining factor, in whether or not a mother can be independent in caring for her child, may depend on the equipment available. Even though it is used for a relatively short time it is worth the effort to select and adapt the equipment to suit the mother's particular needs. This will give her a feeling of independence and self-confidence and the personal satisfaction of knowing that she can assume at least part of her normal role.

In selecting new equipment these questions should be considered:

Is it equipment manageable within the mother's limitations?

Is it adjustable in height? Can it be moved easily? Does it have easily manipulated controls?

Is it suitable for more than one use and over a long period of time? Is it sturdy and durable? Is it adaptable to the rapid growth of the child? Is it easy to care for?

Does it help in promoting early independence in the child?

Is it safe for both the mother and the child?

There is no single piece of equipment suited to a specific disability. Each mother must choose what most effectively meets her particular limitations, her family budget, and her personal desires. If necessary, it may then be adapted to her special needs. Special care should be given to safety; the latches on cribs and play pens should lock securely, be easy to operate, and of the type that can be manipulated by the mother but not by the child.

Work Centers for Caring for Children

Items of equipment should never be selected as single objects but rather in their relationship to the total performance of a task. They should be part of a work center where a specific task can be carried through all of its stages: getting ready, doing the job, and cleanup. Most tasks related to child care can be accomplished with fewer steps, less fatigue and with greater ease and safety if thoughtful planning is done in advance. This applies to not only the bathing of a baby but to food preparation, laundry, cleaning up and all of the other housekeeping tasks.

Since infants are often diapered and dressed wherever they happen to be in the home at different times of the day, simple equipment should be duplicated if possible. Steps can also be saved by having more than one storage area for items that are used frequently, such as diapers.

Check List for Developing Work Centers

1. Is the center located in the most convenient place, with sufficient space to allow free movement of wheelchairs or wheeled carts?
2. Is the equipment arranged for easy flow of work and so as to eliminate lifting from one area to another?
3. Is there adequate storage for materials, tools, and utensils, arranged so as to be easy to see, easy to reach, easy to grasp? If not, have provisions been made for easy ways to transport them by basket, tray, wheeled cart, or some other method?
4. Is the work surface planned at a comfortable height for the person using it? If not, can either the seat or the working surface be adjusted in height?
5. Is there provision for a work surface with adequate knee room for sitting to work for at least part of the job?
6. Is there a seat of comfortable height and depth to allow the person to maintain good body posture?
7. Are working surfaces, storage facilities, and equipment planned to facilitate easy cleanup?
8. Is the equipment used at the center chosen with the limitations of the person's disability in mind, or can it be adapted to suit her special needs?

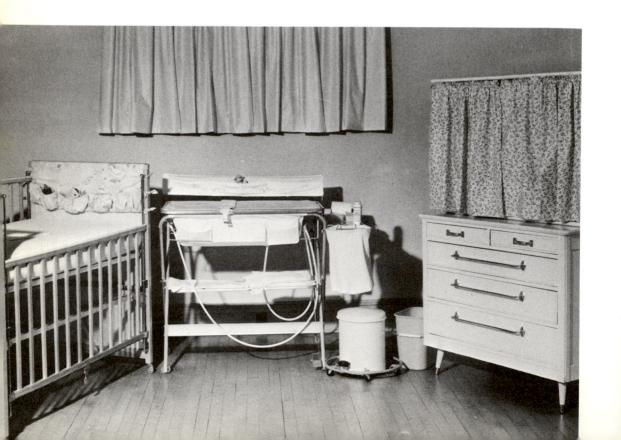

Work Simplification Principles Applied to the Job of Bathing a Baby
By a Mother Limited to the Use of Her Right Hand

Step One: Study the Job to be Done

What is the job?   To bathe and dress the baby.
Who will do it?   The mother wants to do it herself.
When will she do it?   Any time during the day that is most convenient for
                          the mother.
Where will she do it?   Any place she can arrange a comfortable workplace.
How will she do it?   This mother took into account her own physical limitations and the resources of her family in money, time, and skills. She
reduced to a minimum the amount of walking, stooping, stretching, bending, lifting and carrying in order to conserve both time and energy and
yet maintain high standards of safety for her baby and for herself.

Step Two: Selection and Arrangement of Equipment

THE CRIB has an adjustable spring which permits the raising of the mattress
to a comfortable working height. The foot-lever makes it possible to lower
the side of crib to the level of the mattress and leaves the arm free for easier
lifting.

THE BATHINETTE combines a dressing table, tub and clothes storage area. It
includes a foot pedal to raise the table when the mother is ready to transfer
the baby to the tub, a hammock in the tub to support the baby and a hose
to empty the tub easily. The shelf provides easy-to-reach storage for clothes.
A laundry bag is attached.

THE STEP-ON DIAPER PAIL, on a dolly, can be opened easily or moved with the
foot.

THE CLOTHES STORAGE consists of two stacked chests which provide easy to
reach storage, easy to grasp handles and easy to open curtains. Because of
careful planning the mother need never risk leaving her child unguarded.

Step Three: Procedure in Bathing the Baby

Before the bath starts, towels and clean clothes that will be needed are selected and placed within easy reach in the order in which they will be used. The mother uses the "knee to shoulder" height storage for frequently used

items to avoid stooping and stretching. She wears a terry cloth cobbler's apron to protect her dress during the bathing process.

Water of the right temperature is brought from the bathroom in this lightweight plastic rectangular pail which is easy to rest against the tub. The bathinette foot pedal is used to raise the table.

To take the child from the crib she bends her body over the crib and slides her elbow and forearm down to support the baby's back and her hand to support his head. Her entire arm and all of her fingers help to hold the baby safely.

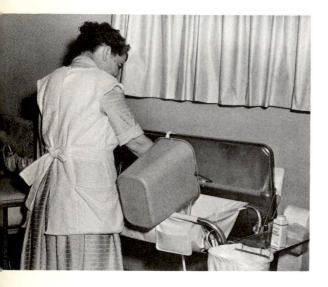

As she undresses the baby, she drops the soiled clothes directly into the laundry bag and the diaper into the diaper pail. This keeps her work area clear.

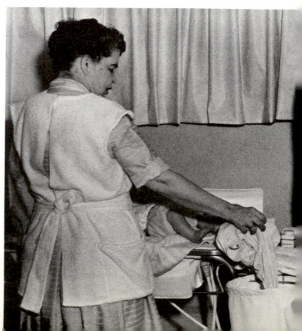

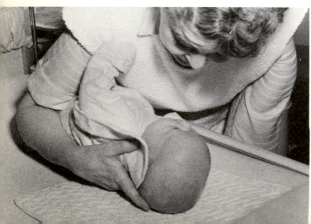

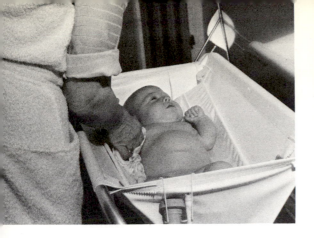

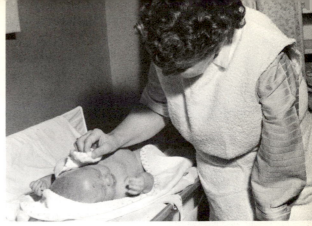

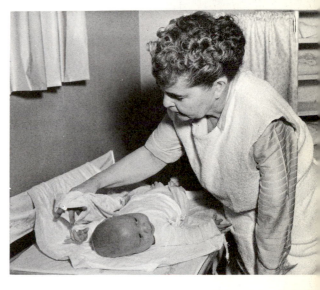

The hammock in the bathinette tub supports the baby in the bath water much as a second hand would do. Carefully selected equipment makes it possible for her to do this job.

After lifting the baby from the bath, she lays him on a towel which was placed on the top of the bathinette before the bathing began. A receiving blanket placed under the towel is ready to place him on for the dressing process. Dot fasteners are used on the diapers.

In dressing the baby, she uses garments that open all the way down the front. She opens the sleeve with her fingers so she can slip it comfortably over the baby's hand. After putting on one sleeve, she slips the garment under his back and rolls him over gently to put on the second sleeve.

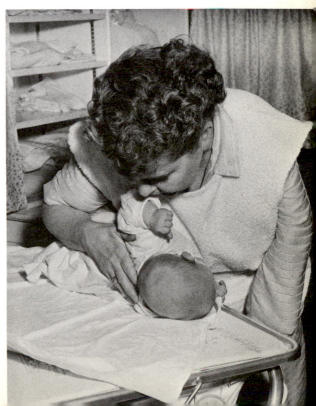

To keep the baby secure when she must step away from the work table to prepare his bed, she fastens the safety belt.

The baby is now ready for bed.

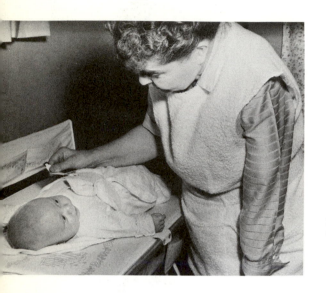

Step Four: Cleanup

To leave the bathinette ready for its next use, she drains the tub into the plastic pail with the gravity drain hose and wipes it clean and dry.

After the tub is drained and wiped clean, and the bath table is down for next use, the storage curtains are closed. The job is accomplished within the limitations of her handicap and with a minimum of walking, stooping, stretching, bending, and lifting.

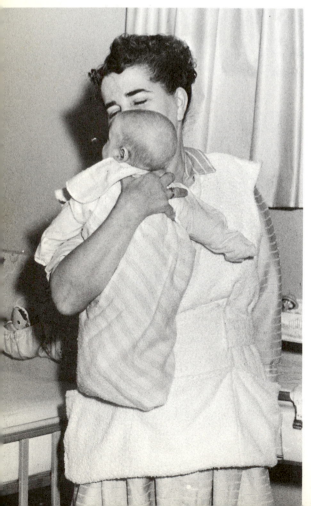

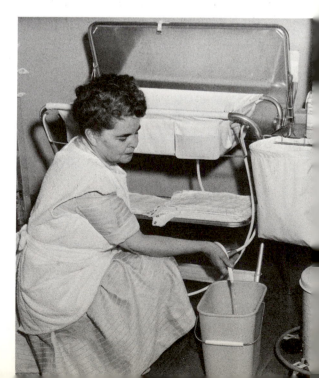

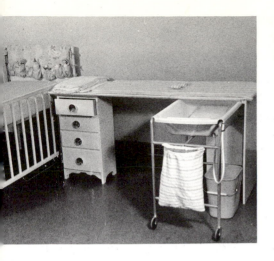
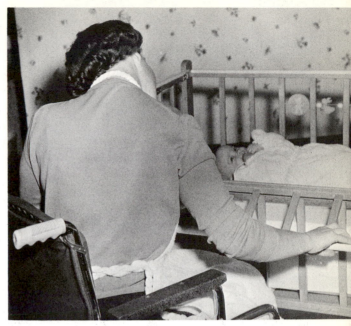

Bathing and Dressing Center
for the Mother Who Sits to Work

Desirable Features

1. ARRANGEMENT.

   Equipment arranged to permit easy flow of work. The baby is transferred from the crib, to the dressing table, to the bath, with a minimum of effort.

2. THE CRIB.

   Wooden frame under mattress raises it to a comfortable height for lifting the baby.

   Side of crib hinged so it may be dropped to make it easier to lift the baby.

45

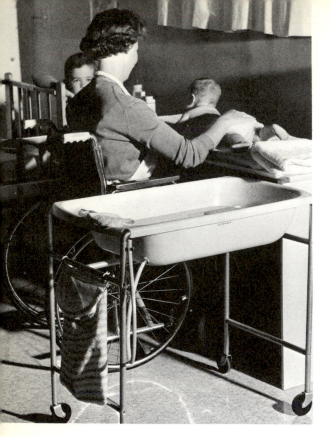

3. DRESSING TABLE. (A)

Easy-to-reach clothing storage.

Easy-to-grasp drawer pulls.

4. BATHING UNIT. (A)

Comfortable working height, with knee room to permit dressing in a forward position.

Standard plastic tub, slanting contour bottom with foam rubber pad to support baby. (Turkish towel may be substituted for foam rubber.)

Light mobile frame for tub, with casters to facilitate filling and draining.

Gravity drain makes it easy to empty.

Tub may be stored under counter when not in use.

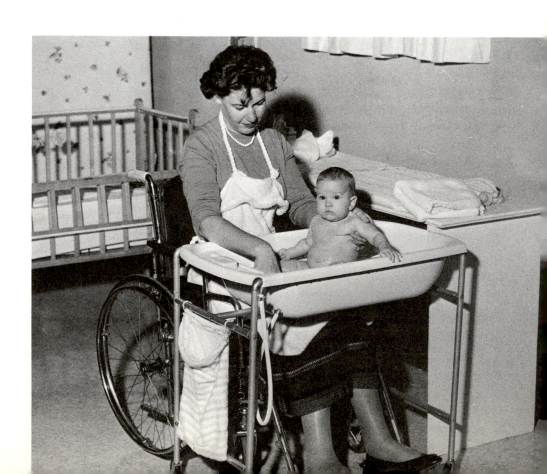

The Kitchen Sink for Baby Bathing (B)

1. ADVANTAGES.

Furnishes sturdy support.

Easy to fill and drain.

Comfortable and safe for mother in wheelchair; when it is lowered to a comfortable height and knee room is provided, the mother can work in a forward position.

May also be used by mother working from a standing position if the height is comfortable.

2. SAFEGUARDS.

Rubber cover on faucet necessary to protect baby's head.

Towel or sponge rubber necessary on bottom of sink or on drainboard to prevent slipping.

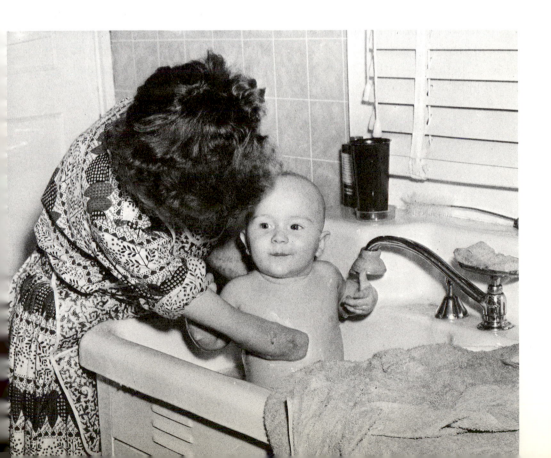

Baby Bathing with Simple Equipment

A Wash Basin on a Card Table

A card table covered with an ordinary bed pad and a bath towel can serve as a bathing and dressing table for a wheelchair mother, since it allows knee room and permits her to work in a forward position. All of the bathing and dressing supplies should be placed on a table or wheeled cart nearby in order of use, before the bath begins. This makes it unnecessary for the mother to leave the baby unguarded.

The Family Bathtub for Baby Bathing

The conventional family bathtub has proved to be hazardous for many people and is ordinarily avoided by mothers with physical limitations when bathing very young children. There are a few advantages, however, in that bathtubs are easy to fill and drain. Some mothers manage by sitting close to the tub on a low stool with non-skid pads on the legs, or better still on a hassock that will not tip or skid. A small plastic tub set inside the family tub is sometimes used.

Safety precautions are necessary for anyone using a bathtub. Always place a towel or, better still, a rubber mat held by suction cups in the bottom of the tub to prevent slipping. Install grab bars on both sides of the tub within the reach of children, or anyone else using the tub. Raise tub to a more convenient height if possible. Teach the child safety measures as early as possible. A bath seat with a safety strap and suction cups sometimes makes it possible to bathe young children in the tub.

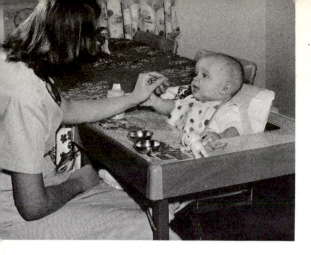

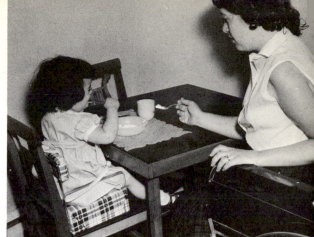

Feeding Tables and Chairs

Feeding Tables

Strain is diminished if the legs of the feeding table can be extended to allow knee room for the mother to work in a forward position.

Highchairs

Highchairs bring the child to the level of the family table. Trays that can be released on one side of the chair and dropped on the other, have advantages for the mother with hand limitations.

Chair Seats for Children

When the child grows older, a small seat on an adult-size chair will raise him to table height.

The Selection of Feeding Equipment

Bottles, Nipples, Formulas

Wide-mouthed bottles are easier to clean and to fill. Nipples with caps that screw on are easier to manage than those that pull on. Bottles may be heat-proof glass, plastic, or disposable bottles. Pre-sterilized formula preparations in disposable cans and bottles are now available. All formula preparations, must of course, be checked with a physician.

Safety Precautions for Highchairs and Feeding Tables

Adjustable foot rest adds to the child's comfort and safety.

Locking devices must be dependable and easy to manipulate.

Trays should be easy to clean.

Safety straps provided by the manufacturer are sometimes difficult for a person with hand involvements to operate. A dog leash snap fastened to a homemade strap of soft cotton webbing may be easier to manage.

A combination of roomy pants attached to a slip cover which may be put over the back of the high chair, prevents the child from slipping through. (A)

The Selection of Toileting Equipment

Advantages and disadvantages should be considered before purchasing.

Points to Consider

1. TOILET SEAT TO FIT OVER CONVENTIONAL TOILET

Is it sturdy and well made?

Does it fasten easily and securely without tilting and furnish the support needed?

Can he climb up to it safely with the help of a stool or can someone lift him?

Will the toilet seat fold easily for storage?

2. TOILET CHAIRS

When the child is very young a toilet chair may be put on a low table or platform if the mother has difficulty in bending.

When the toilet chair is on floor level the child may be able to use it by himself.

A single purpose toilet chair makes toilet training easier.

A folding toilet chair can be easily transported and avoids interrupting toilet training in travel.

A plastic portable urinal with a lid is useful for small boys. A very young child can be taught to use the urinal alone and can also learn to empty it properly.

Plastic Seats for Infants

Portable plastic seats for infants are well padded and include a safety strap. This device offers stability for feeding and transporting a baby.

50

The Selection of a Play Pen

Points to Consider

What size will fit into the space available? Will it be necessary to fold it when not in use? Is it sturdy enough to be moved about and to withstand rough wear? Is it safe for the child; are catches, bolts, hinges and locks of the type that a child cannot operate or cannot pinch his fingers? Are the sides such that he cannot climb over? Can the person caring for the child operate the locks? Can the child be lifted in and out of the play pen without undue strain?

PLAY PENS WITH FOLD-DOWN SIDES. The fold-down side reduces the height and makes it possible for the wheelchair mother to lift her child in and out and also to clean the pen more easily.

MESH-TYPE PLAY PENS. The side of the mesh-type play pen can be let down easily. The pen folds easily and can also be used as a bed. The mesh is fairly "climb-proof."

RAISED PLAY PENS. A mother limited to the use of one arm, and with difficulty in bending, will find a floor level play pen impossible to use. The problem may be solved by extending the legs and raising the level to approximately 27 inches. A gate cut in the side makes it much easier to reach in to lift the baby. This same adaptation may have advantages for a mother confined to a wheelchair (A).

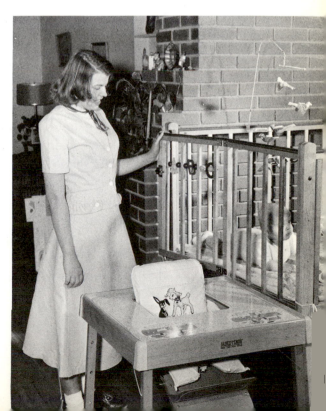

Clothes for Infants

Mothers will have fewer problems if when they select baby's clothes, they remember that comfort for the baby, and convenience for the mother, are the primary concerns. Beyond the essentials of diapers, shirts and sleeping garments there are the frills. These may create dressing or care problems, but may give the mother great satisfaction. Clothing that can be opened flat, so the baby can be placed easily into the garment, are a great advantage in dressing and in changing diapers.

General Suggestions for Buying Infants' Wear

A. DIAPERS may be selected in different fabrics, sizes and shapes. The most important quality is the absorbency but there are other factors to consider, such as fastening, drying time and styles which might help mother to save her energy and time. If a commercial diaper service is available and is approved by the physician, it would certainly be worth considering.

Fabric Choices

Gauze: light weight, non-bulky, absorbent, quick-drying.
Stretch Gauze: all the qualities of regular gauze plus stretch to fit.
Birdseye: heavier but durable and absorbent diaper fabric, slower to dry than gauze.
Knitted: very absorbent, holds shape well but slower to dry, stretches to fit.
Disposable: soft, absorbent layers of non-woven cellulosic material. Some have special layer that draws wetness away from liner next to baby's skin. Outside layer of plastic prevents moisture from seeping through layers.

Design Choices

Square or rectangular shapes (27"x27" or 21"x40") can be folded to give maximum protection.
Prefolded styles save time and energy.
Tubular styles stretch easily to fit and eliminate folding.
Contour styles are shaped to fit and are adjustable around the waist and in length.
Disposable diapers are shaped, prefolded or flat styles, with adhesive tapes for easy fastening.
Diaper liners used inside cloth diapers are made of a knitted material that does not hold moisture. They add to comfort especially during sleeping periods. Some are disposable and made of non-woven fabrics.

B. PROTECTIVE PANTIES are made in a number of styles and a variety of fabrics. A style that opens flat will permit easier dressing and quick diaper changes with less handling. These are not necessary if disposable diapers are used.

C. SHIRTS. Snap-front or snap-side (double breasted) knitted shirts are easy to put on and fasten. Shirts are available with short or long sleeves and are made of blends of polyester and cotton or all cotton. Slip-on styles should have an overlap in the shoulder area to make dressing easier and more comfortable for baby.

D. KIMONOS OR NIGHTGOWNS are the traditional infants' garment. They are usually made of soft, smooth knitted fabrics and are easy to put on because they open flat or have long snap openings. One-piece stretch sleepers with feet and center front openings that extend into the leg area are popular all-purpose garments for infants. The size of stretch garments must be checked often to be sure there is adequate room for movement and growth.

E. SWEATERS AND SACQUES should open all the way down the front and have raglan sleeves for adequate growing room and easy dressing.

F. BUNTINGS are a good choice for outdoor wear because they keep the baby comfortably warm. It is easier to handle a baby in a bunting than one wrapped in a blanket. There are two styles: One is like an envelope with a hood. The baby is completely covered except for his face. The other style is two-pieced and has, in addition, a jacket top with long sleeves and attached mittens. The bunting must be large enough to allow room for the baby to move easily. Some buntings have "growth tucks" so they can be lengthened as the child grows, or a bunting may be converted into a bootee suit.

G. BIBS made of absorbent material are most satisfactory. The point to check is the method of fastening. Velcro may sometimes be substituted for ties.

H. BONNETS, CAPS, AND HOODS. Simple styles with side fasteners are to be preferred to those that tie under the chin. The comfort of the child and the convenience of the mother are primary concerns.

I. BOOTIES AND SOCKS. For warmth, knee socks have advantages over booties.

CHAPTER 5

Developing Early Independence and Cooperative Behavior in Young Children

The task of bringing up children is a complex problem for all parents, and they are sure to have doubts and uncertainties. For the mother with physical limitations, this feeling of inadequacy is amplified. She may question her ability to perform the necessary tasks, to meet emergencies, and to find the best ways to guide the growth and development of her children. Her self-confidence may suffer even more if other family members question whether she is equal to this responsibility.

Judging from the experience of the mothers who contributed ideas to this book, physical limitations need not be a bar to being a good mother. The fact that she must stay at home may even have its advantages. Children develop a sense of security because they know they can count on her being there when they need her. Since she cannot depend on strength and speed

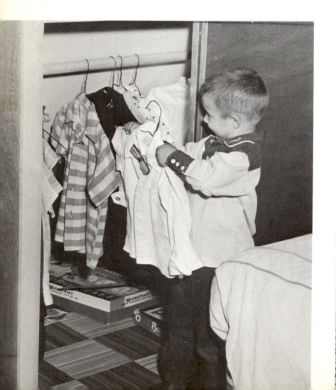

to enforce obedience, a handicapped mother must build a basic trust between herself and her children and win cooperative behavior. This will challenge her patience, her imagination, and her ingenuity.

The development of cooperative behavior may begin at any age, but it is a gradual process. Parents must understand what is reasonable to expect of a child at each stage of his development. If he is physically able to do a task, and if he wants to do it, he should be encouraged to do it regardless of his age. Success in one activity will help him to develop the skill and self-confidence he needs to do more difficult tasks.

The Importance of Play Activities

Since play activities fill most of the child's day, it is important for the parent to take advantage of the opportunities they offer for developing initiative, creativeness, unselfishness, cooperativeness, gentleness, kindness, and many other desirable traits. This chapter suggests activities which children may share with adults or with other children, along with those which they may carry on independently.

Since young children enjoy being near their mothers, it is wise to have small play centers in each of the rooms where the mother is likely to spend a considerable amount of her time. Such areas can be more easily supervised than a separate game room and offer more opportunity for friendly companionship between the mother and her children.

Outdoor Play Supervised from the Indoors

The problem of giving children the opportunity for free outdoor play is not an easy one for a handicapped mother. One mother worked out a clever plan by fencing in a play area adjoining the house so that it can be supervised from the window or doorway. The only entrance is through the house. This is a safety factor and also gives her control over the number of children who use the play area at one time. She invites the neighbors' children to use the yard, and in exchange, their mothers often include her children on trips where she would find it impossible to take them.

If a yard can include a driveway, children can use their tricycles and other wheel toys. A grassy spot with climbing equipment is another fine feature, and a sand box or a place for digging makes the place ideal.

By using a ramp some parents can join their children in outdoor games. Many ball games do not require running, and anyone with a good voice can be an umpire even though he is in a wheelchair. Storytelling, nature study, dramatics, music, and crafts are only a few of the activities where parents in wheelchairs can join in children's play (I-22).

Outdoor Play Equipment

A great assortment of outdoor equipment may be purchased but much of it can be built at home (I-22). Problems of

safety are the first concern. Some pieces, such as a trampoline, can be very dangerous and should not be used without direct supervision and strict regulations.

The Sand Box

The sand box is probably the most popular piece of equipment and can be a place where children learn to share and to respect each other's rights. If children help to make the rules governing the sand box, they are more likely to follow them.

The simplest sand box is made of four logs used to enclose a heap of sand. If the sand box has a floor with small drain holes and is raised off the ground, the sand is more likely to stay dry. Corners made of boards provide seats and are also a good place to put out molds of cupcakes and sand pies. Simple household equipment free from sharp edges or pointed ends is good for sand box play—cans with smooth edges, muffin pans, pie pans, large spoons, scoops, sifters, or flower pots.

A sand box with wheels has advantages, since it can be moved to sun or shade or even into the garage on a rainy day. A canopy is fine for shade and can sometimes be used as a cover when the box is not in use. In any case, the box should have a waterproof cover to protect it from the weather, and also from stray cats!

Water Play

Plastic pools are fun, but large dishpans and old-fashioned wash tubs can be used instead, or a sprinkler, or simply going out in a warm rain.

Another idea for outdoor fun is to use just plain water as though it were paint. With a man-sized brush a child can paint the fence, the steps, or almost anything. Blowing soap bubbles is more fun out of doors than indoors, since there is no need for being careful of dripping.

Something to Swing On

A satellite swing is fine, but a rubber tire or a rope with a knot or a small board can provide the same fun. A tree with just the right limb is a good place to hang an old-fashioned rope swing.

Something to Climb On

Slides and jungle gyms may be purchased, but a good substitute can be made from a sturdy ladder that is well supported at the ends and placed just high enough to be grasped by jumping.

Something to Rock On

Rocking teeter-boards can be purchased, but a simple one can be made of a plank over a solid center support like a sawhorse, or it may be supported on the axle between two old wagon wheels.

Active Indoor Play

Since children need activity and are sure to be noisy some of the time, there must be some arrangement in every home for active play. A wise mother soon learns that noise can be tolerated more easily if she plays with her children.

An *indoor gym* provides for many different activities and takes little space. Various pieces of equipment may be attached to a single hanger on a door frame (I-22). This can be left in position when equipment is not in use. Even a three-year-old can add a great deal to his skill and self-confidence by mastering the task of adjusting equipment to his own height. A child as young as eighteen months can climb a swinging ladder. A small slide placed on the end of a sofa or chair gives a toddler an opportunity for hours of fun and good exercise. (H—Child Life and Play Specialty Assoc.)

Select Safe Toys for Children

Because of his short interest span, a child will need several toys, but he should not be overloaded. Toys should have more than one use; those a child can either play with alone or with other children are good investments. The price of the toy is not necessarily an indication of its worth.

Since a handicapped mother may be limited in her ability to meet emergencies, it is important for her to give special attention to safety in selecting toys. Here are points to consider:

1. SIZE. They should be too large to put into mouth, nose, or ears.
2. DECORATIONS. Avoid small decorations that can come off and be swallowed, such as button eyes on animals, bells, small wheels.
3. CONSTRUCTION. Look for sturdy construction that cannot be taken apart and that will tolerate rough wear without breaking. Avoid sharp edges or pointed ends.
4. WASHABILITY. Avoid hairy toys that might lose their fur and those that are not completely washable.
5. PAINT. Be sure toys are painted with non-toxic paint. Paints containing lead compounds may be poisonous to children.
6. HANDLES. All handles on push-pull toys should be protected with a large knob or bar.

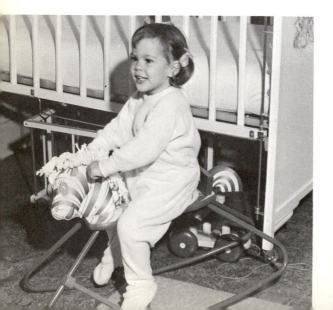

Safety Gates

Since the handicapped parent may not be able to move quickly to rescue the child from accidents, safety gates are a necessity to close off all stairways or rooms the parent cannot supervise. A folding extendable type which is fastened to the door frame is usually satisfactory. One should be sure the lock can be manipulated by the parent but not by the child.

Storage of Toys

Each toy ought to have a special storage place of its own. Learning to take care of his toys is an important part of a child's training; if he is old enough to get them out, he is old enough to put them away! A child does not have an adult attitude toward neatness and order. He will need a convenient and logical space with plenty of room for storage, and a considerable amount of guidance and encouragement. Only a few toys should be out at one time. If the space where each toy is to be stored is marked out with crayon, the child will learn to put things where they belong.

A toy cart, which a very young child can pull, is especially valuable in a home where a mother has difficulty in picking up things from the floor. For a toddler, the handle of the cart should go across the entire end so that it is easier to maneuver in a small space. A cart equipped with bells makes it easier for a parent to know where the child is playing. A cardboard box with a clothesline rope handle makes a good temporary cart.

61

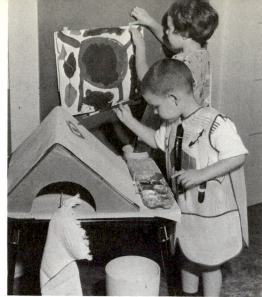

Homemade Playthings

Children often have much more fun with homemade toys that *merely suggest an idea* than they do with commercial toys complete in every detail. Here are some simple ideas:

BEGIN WITH A BOX. Add cardboard wings and it's an airplane. Add paddles and make a boat. Add a steering wheel and some coffee cans for headlights and it's a car. Cut in windows and doors and it's a house or a garage. Tie on some clothesline for a handle and it's a sled, a wagon, or a toy cart. Add rockers and it's a doll cradle. Add a roof, a tin can for a silo, and it's a barn.

BEGIN WITH A RUBBER TIRE. (Spar varnish keeps black from rubbing off.) Suspend it with a rope from a tree and use it as a swing. Suspend two of them from a low limb and put a board between them for a low swing. Fill the center section of a large tire with sand to make a sand pile for a young child.

BEGIN WITH A HOMEMADE EASEL. (To make the easel, cut a box in half to form a triangle, and put it on a table.) Provide paper, chalk, or water color and brush, and let imaginations take over from then on!

BEGIN WITH A ROPE. Tie a loop in one end, tie it to a limb, and you have a rope to climb. Tie the two ends securely over a stout limb, add a board notched on each side for a seat, and you have a swing.

CHAPTER 6

Music, Dramatics, Art, and Nature Study for Young Children to Share with Parents and Grandparents

Sharing Musical Experiences

Music in all of its forms offers a wonderful opportunity for parents and children to join together in something that is fun to do. Suitable musical instruments present the child with an opportunity to experiment with sounds. Many "toy" instruments are disappointing to children because they cannot be accurately tuned and the sound is often unpleasant.

Homemade Instruments

Children learn something of sound and rhythm from simple devices. A pie tin does not sound too loud if it is pounded with a padded stick. Clothespins in a cardboard carton make a wonderful rattle. Children learn different kinds of sounds and rhythms, by drumming on cans or cartons of various sizes.

Some children enjoy keeping time when music is being played. If the parent can demonstrate the possibilities, they learn to experiment with fast and slow rhythms and with loud and soft sounds.

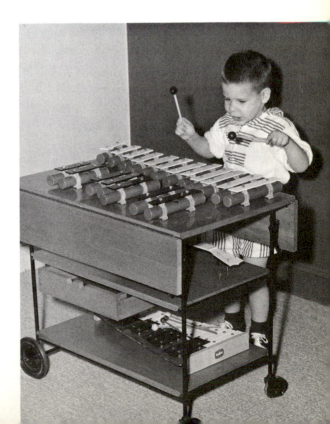

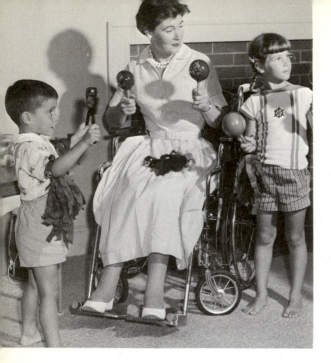

Playing Musical Instruments

If someone can show the child how the piano works and play for him, his haphazard banging on the keyboard will give way to thoughtful experimentation. Those who have been fortunate enough to be a part of a family orchestra know what joy the experience can be. Very young children can learn to develop rhythm and melody. They can be taught at a very early age to respect instruments and to use them properly.

Singing Together

The warm family associations built around singing are more important than the songs that are sung. A feeling of comradeship and family harmony can often come from singing together even when washing dishes or doing other routine jobs or riding in the family car.

Listening Together

"High fidelity" music is important for children, too. Poor recordings actually defeat the purpose for which they are made. Very young children can be taught how to be careful in handling record players. This can open up a whole new area of music for them. They can listen to records, dance to records, and sing to records. Let them be independent in choosing and playing. Favorites can be identified by different pictures pasted on the records until the child is old enough to read.

Art Materials for Children

The chief value in using art materials is to help the child develop skill and self-confidence and give him an opportunity for self-expression through creative play. Only simple equipment and materials are needed, such as clay, finger paint, blocks, water color, chalk, crayons, scissors and paper, nails and wood. But tools and equipment alone are not enough. The parent must set the limits on when and where the materials can be used and instruct the child on how to use them.

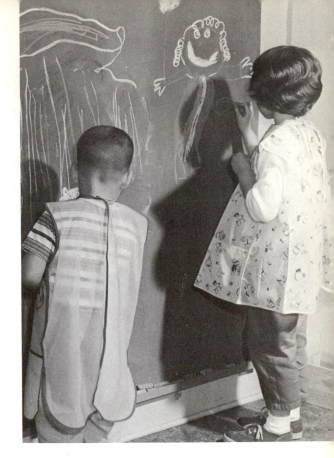

Blackboards, Chalk, and Crayons

A good-sized blackboard along with a supply of white and colored chalk can provide a wonderful opportunity for creative play. With a damp sponge and just a little help on how to use it, a young child can have the fun of washing off one picture and starting another.

Chalk can be used in a variety of ways: it makes wonderful bright lines on wet paper; if it is grated, it will color starch paste; if the chalk is dipped into a little water, it can be used to make designs on any kind of cloth as well as on paper.

Crayons are fun, too, and allow for growth in skill and imagination and creativeness, provided they *are not used in coloring books*. Little fingers do not have the coordination necessary to "stay within the lines," and it does nothing for a child's imagination to color a picture someone else had the fun of making. Choose lightweight, soft, wax crayons that make a broad line of bright color. Crayons work well on cloth, and young children love to make play aprons, Indian suits, or decorate old sheets for dress-up. If the cloth is ironed on the wrong side, the color becomes fairly permanent.

Water-Color Paint

Jars of ready-mixed poster paints can be purchased, but it is cheaper to buy dry powdered paint and help the child mix his own colors (F). When a child starts to paint, there should be no pattern for him to follow. He will soon learn to experiment and will have the fun of combining colors. A variety of brushes will please him. Let him try an old toothbrush dipped into paint. If this is raked across a piece of window screening, it will give him a spattered effect. A piece of sponge or a wad of cotton will make interesting spots that will add to the fun. Empty thread spools, when dipped into paint, will add another variation. Small bottle tops may be used in the same way.

Finger Painting

Finger painting is fun for any age group. It involves no tools and requires no mastery of skills. It is relaxing and stimulates the imagination; it improves coordination and offers an opportunity to learn much about color.

There are some commercial finger paints that are harmless to the skin and clothing, but the homemade recipe works well too (F). Allow enough space for finger painting so that the child can have plenty of freedom of movement. A small easel at comfortable height is best, but a table can be used.

66

Playing with Paste and Glue and a Stapler

Paste may be purchased or made at home (F). If children have some direction for applying it, they can work creatively for many hours. Some five-year-olds are able to manage airplane glue and construct such things as log cabins, towers, and fences from toothpicks.

Free-Hand Cutting

An investment in a good pair of *blunt-pointed* scissors for a child who has learned the limits, can be a source of great pleasure. Children may need help in learning how to hold scissors, but even two-year-olds often have sufficient muscular coordination to use them successfully.

After the child learns to use a stapler and understands how to make a box, a cylinder, and a triangle, he has the basis for a great variety of constructive ideas. When he learns to cut reasonably straight lines, he can weave strips of color together for table mats or carpets for the dollhouse.

Fun with Clay

Because of its mobility, clay is ideal for creative activity. Even if he makes nothing at all, he will play contentedly with clay for a long time.

Work with Wood

A stout wooden box makes a good base for a workbench. If the child has tools of good quality and suited to his age, he can soon construct a variety of toys. A vise is important, so that boards may be held firmly when they are sawed. He should have a supply of scraps of soft pine boards and roofing nails with large heads and, to begin with, a wooden mallet rather than a metal hammer. Heavy cardboard can be sawed easily and is good for construction. Any water color paint will help to dress up the finished product.

Creative Experience Through Storytelling

With the widespread use of "canned amusement" in radio and television, storytelling has been neglected in many homes. A story told, with or without a book to lean on, can be stimulating to a child's imagination and bring the parent and child into a closer relationship. Through storytelling parents may share experiences and stress values that are important to them.

Story telling is one of the creative experiences where it is easy to acquire the necessary skill. Memorizing a story is not necessary nor is it important to have a special time or place for storytelling. Let the stories be based on the child's own experience and on the questions he asks. When he asks, "Why?", "How?" "Where?" "What makes it go?" or "What will it be like?" the parent has the basis for a story. He will be interested in stories of his parents' childhood, "When I was a little girl" or "When daddy was a boy."

Children should be encouraged to tell stories of their own, both true and fanciful. Parents should take time to listen and ask to have special stories told over again. Children will love to share their interests and experiences, and a wise parent can learn a great deal about the development of the children by the stories they tell.

Tell a Story Together

Children enjoy taking turns in telling a story. The parent may start the story and then when the child is ready, let him carry it along. It becomes a game to have one pick up the story where the other leaves off.

Another suggestion for story telling is to have everyone try to be very quiet and listen, and then tell a story about whatever they hear but cannot see. It might be the sound of rain on the roof or the barking of a dog, or a train whistle, or a bullfrog in the pond. Some of the sounds they have heard may be imitated and used in the story. This game can be played indefinitely any time, any place.

Sing a Story Together

Another way to have fun with stories is to sing a story together. It merely means that you sing whatever you would normally say. With a simple rhythm which is easy to follow, the parent and child can sing a part. "This is the way we iron our clothes," "Leave your ironing and come to lunch," "When you have finished, please feed the kitty." This can go on indefinitely and can be accompanied by pantomime.

Play the Story

It is fairly easy to shift from storytelling to playing the role of one of the characters in the story. In telling a story about Indians, it is easy to dress up by merely adding a feather and a blanket. Simple costume accessories combine naturally with storytelling. A costume box may provide excitement for many a rainy day.

Illustrate Stories with Cut-outs

Illustrations can be cut from construction paper and pasted on a plain surface to illustrate a story, but it is more satisfactory to cut simple figures from scraps of felt and build your story as you go along. Cut-outs of felt stick best to felt-like surfaces such as the back of dining table pads or even an old army blanket.

Stories from Scrapbooks

The scrapbook of pictures offers a simple way to pin down, organize, and extend a child's ideas. Old magazines furnish an infinite number of pictures to cut out. A child can make a book of the things he wants for Christmas, or various kinds of animals, flowers, or birds.

Stories in Rhyme

Young children love nonsense rhymes that mean little but are fun to say. If a parent begins with "The cat is fat," the child may come back with "He sat and sat." It can always end with "Just think of that." Such experiences help to enlarge the child's vocabulary and increase his skill in expressing himself.

Make a Big Picture

Try putting some wrapping paper on the wall and let the child play he is taking a trip. He can cut and paste all of the things he thinks will be involved in the trip, modes of travel, things he will see, and the people he will meet. In making his own big picture, he has an excellent opportunity to tell and illustrate his own story.

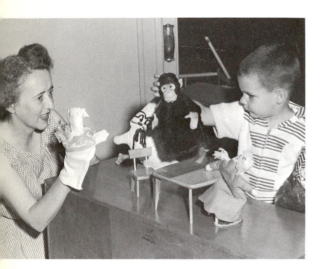

Let Puppets Tell the Story

Puppets of wood, bottles, paper bags, or mitten-type hand puppets are easy for young children to use in retelling stories. A simple stage made of a cardboard carton, or simply a table top, answers the purpose. Very simple hand puppets can be made of scraps of material, yarn, and embroidery floss. With some directions and encouragement, a child can enlarge his concept of other personalities and other situations through dramatic play.

DRAMATIC PLAY allows the child to play a role other than himself

Stories from Books

Picture books and illustrated stories help the very young child in learning new words and in associating these with objects or situations. As he grows older, he will enjoy many kinds of stories. By introducing the child to the world of books, a parent can start him out on a lifetime of pleasure and self-education. What to choose depends on the child's development and interests.

Points to consider in selecting a book for a child:

Is it wholesome and worthwhile in its content?

Are the ideas well expressed?

Is it likely to fit in with the child's interests or develop new ones?

Is it something the child wants himself?

Is it well printed, well illustrated, and durable?

With the proper encouragement, children can learn from the beginning to respect books, to keep them clean and to avoid damaging them in any way.

Explore the Outdoors Indoors

Even though a mother can no longer walk in the woods or wade in a stream with her children, she can still open their eyes and ears to the mystery, the wonder, and the beauty of growing things. Children can be inspired by such simple experiences as watching a robin raise her brood, or by seeing a narcissus bulb grow leaves and flowers, or by learning to recognize a few of the stars. In this way a child may develop some appreciation of the laws that govern the universe. These are interests and appreciations which can be shared for a life time by children and adults of all ages.

A good way to teach children to be thoughtful and gentle is to give them a first-hand contact with living things. Children should never be allowed to pick flowers unless they expect to put them into water and care for them. They should never pull flowers apart, merely in order to have something to do. They can develop a sensitiveness and concern for helpless little creatures by taking care of those that might accidentally stray into the house or that might be in danger of being crushed on a sidewalk. A cricket can be pushed gently onto a piece of paper and given his freedom. A butterfly that might have strayed indoors will cling to a stick and can then be released. Children can be taught the difference between the necessity for destroying creatures that are doing some damage, such as flies, mosquitoes and mice, and the importance of giving freedom to those who are doing no harm.

An interest in living things can be the basis of many true stories that can be shared with children. For example, they can easily learn to recognize a robin and to become acquainted with his song, but that is only a beginning. They will also love stories about what the robin eats, where he lives in summer, where he goes in the wintertime, what he uses to make his nest, the number and color of his eggs and perhaps why we should protect him. There are many stories in the life history of insects. Take, for example, the astonishing life of a butterfly; the mating flight, the laying of eggs, the hatching of the baby caterpillars, their amazing appetites and rapid growth, the weaving of a cocoon, and finally the emerging of the butterfly from the cocoon. These science stories are sometimes more interesting to a child than fairy stories.

A great deal of excellent teaching material in the field of nature study is now available at nominal cost, through such organizations as The National Audubon Society, the American Museum of Natural History and The National Recreation Association. Many communities now have bird clubs where children and adults share common interests (H).

74

Plants for Indoors and Outdoors

The cultivation of plants by young children can be the beginning of developing sensitivity to and an awareness of beauty. Some parents never permit children to destroy flowers or tear them apart or even pick them unless they expect to care for them properly (I-102.) (A great deal of material on the growing of plants is available in every state from the State Agricultural College.)

Many homes provide a small garden plot for children beginning as early as three years old. This can be safely supervised from the window if there is a good cooperative relationship between the parent and the child. With a little sunshine and moisture, almost any soil will grow a few radishes or a little lettuce or even a few pansy plants. More ambitious gardens require special attention to the soil, to moisture and drainage. The important thing is to limit whatever is attempted to plants which are likely to bring success.

In addition to the outdoor garden, children enjoy window boxes on the outside or the inside of the windows. Some vegetables and fruit seeds sprout well indoors. Carrots cut about an inch below the top and placed in water grow into pretty green plants. A sweet potato suspended halfway in a glass by using toothpicks will grow a green vine. A damp sponge rolled in grass seed will soon grow a green coat. Parents can teach their children how roots and leaves grow from a seed by sprouting beans or corn in a glass filled with damp cotton.

A "Visitor's House" for Small Animals and Insects

Most of the creatures that live out of doors should stay indoors for only a little while. It is far better to leave them outside than to bring them indoors and allow them to die of neglect.

All children love to bring things from the outdoors and within reasonable limits, parents should welcome this as an opportunity for sharing new interests. They must be aware, however, of the need for careful and cooperative planning.

The companionship of a cat or dog can mean much to a child, but there are also many other small creatures that make good pets. The important thing is to be certain, before the pets are acquired, that they, along with their offspring, if any, can be well cared for (I-97, 100, 104).

CHAPTER 7

The Selection and Adaptation of Clothing to Suit Particular Needs for Men, Women, and Children

Before clothing is purchased, the particular needs of the individual should be studied. Consider these questions: What will make dressing easier? What will help him to look his best? Will it be comfortable? Will it be easy to care for? Will it help to disguise his disability? (I-1-7)

Independence in Dressing

A person limited in the use of his arms, hands, or shoulders may be tempted to take the easy way and allow someone else to dress him. Learning to be independent takes time, patience, and a substantial amount of fortitude as well as the cooperation of family and friends. "Independence" and "courage" are related words and so are "dependence" and "discouragement"!

There is such a thing as being too independent. The degree of disability may determine how much a person can do for himself.

Easy-on, Easy-off Features

Dressing is much easier when garments are easy to put on and take off, such as:

a. Garment openings that are large enough to slip in and out of without struggling.

b. Clothes amply cut through fitted areas, such as the armhole and waistline.

c. Fasteners that are easy to manipulate and located within easy reach.

Easy-to-Fasten Features

The *type*, *size*, and *location* of fasteners on the garment determine how easily they can be managed.

Easy pull tabs

ZIPPERS are easy to pull up or down. Large zipper tabs are easy to grasp and may be made of a fabric loop or metal ring. It is possible to prevent catching by placing an extra piece of fabric to act as a guard under the zipper. Nylon coil zippers are pliable and less likely to snag. If something does get caught, it can be released by folding the zipper together and twisting it apart. Nylon zippers will melt easily and must not be touched with a hot iron.

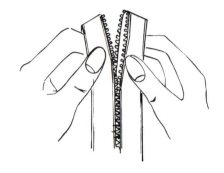

Releasing zipper by folding and pulling apart

BUTTONS must be large enough to grasp and should not be sewed on tightly. A flat, smooth button slips through a buttonhole more easily than a fancy one.

A thread shank on flat buttons makes it easier to grasp the button.

MAGNETIC FASTENERS are relatively new on the market and have been used primarily on children's clothing. They are sure to have more extensive use, since they require little skill to fasten. A tiny magnet snaps the fastener together and very little force is necessary to pull it apart.

79

VELCRO—A type of tape fastener—requires a minimum amount of hand and finger dexterity to open or close the tape. Velcro is two strips of nylon with rough surfaces that stick together like burrs stick to clothing. One side of the tape is made of tiny nylon hooks and the other side has a looped surface. When the two strips come in contact with one another, they lock and hold fast. They unlock by pulling the strips apart.

Since Velcro is made of nylon, it should not be exposed to high temperatures in washing or ironing. Since the loops pick up lint, close the fastener before washing or dry cleaning the garment.

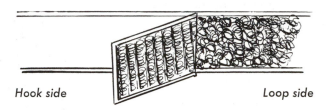

Hook side   *Loop side*

HOOKS AND EYES are difficult to fasten unless they are large and sturdy. The type of metal hook and bar used on men's trousers is more manageable on skirts and slacks for anyone with hand limitations.

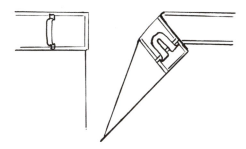

GRIPPERS are usually easier to unfasten than they are to fasten. They require considerable pressure to close.

The *location* of fasteners has a great deal to do with ease in dressing. They should be easy to see, easy to reach, easy to grasp. When located in the center front, they are usually easier to manipulate than on the side or on the back of a garment.

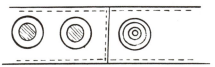

a. Boxy jacket disguises a protruding hip

b. Straight non-fitted waist disguises rib cage

Clothing Can Help a Person to Look His Best

Everyone has certain good features and bad features. Through careful selection of clothing it is possible to emphasize the good ones and play down those which tend to detract from a person's appearance. By making the most of natural assets, and by giving careful attention to grooming, a person can increase his self-confidence, boost his morale, and be an inspiration to those around him.

A good way to begin is to analyze one's appearance and to consider strong points and weak points. Is the figure well proportioned? Is there more length from the waist to the knee than there is from the shoulder to the waist? Are the shoulders and hips approximately the same width? If there are obvious deviations in proportions, then clothing should be selected with lines or colors that will disguise these irregularities. Clothes can give added length or width where it is needed. Clothes can lead the eye up to attractive facial features and focus attention there rather than on the disability.

a. *Pleats in back of shirts give added room.*

b. *Pleat at center back of blouse gives added room.*

c. *Jacket with side pleats released for added room.*

Clothing That Is Comfortable to Wear

Clothes That Allow for Body Movement

To be comfortable clothing must move with the body. The sleeve that binds, the collar that is too tight or the crotch that is too short cannot be ignored; it may be endured, but it will be a constant source of irritation.

The amount of ease that is needed to move comfortably is controlled by the cut of the garment or the way the fabric was made. Action pleats and tucks provide additional fabric for ease and greater freedom of motion. Raglan and kimono sleeves have more room for shoulder movement than regular set-in sleeves.

Stretch fabrics of either woven or knit construction move with the body because such fabrics are capable of stretching beyond their original dimension and recovering most of their shape when strain is released. Many of these fabrics are referred to as comfort stretch because they have enough stretch (10 to 15 percent) to give better fit and shape retention to garments.

82

Easy-to-Adjust Features

A well designed garment should adjust easily to the body and fall into place without excessive pulling or tugging. A blouse or shirt should allow room through the armhole area for ease in getting in and out of the garment. The extra room should allow the garment to "set well" on the shoulders and not "slip off" or "ride back."

Coats should fit well through the shoulder area and be shaped to hug the neck whether worn open or closed. Trousers and skirts should hang smoothly over the hip and thigh area; and should have enough ease to permit a person to sit down and get up without having to readjust them. When these garments are too snug and fit the figure too closely, they have a tendency to wrinkle, twist and "ride up." Garments that hug the waistline closely wrinkle easily and if too tight, may be uncomfortable. Most dresses hang better when there is slight ease through the waist. However, too much ease around the waist of trousers and skirts or shorts will cause them to shift on the body and hang from the hip rather than from the waist. This may create wrinkles and cupping under the buttocks as well as uneven hemlines.

Clothes Sized to Fit

Clothing that is sized to fit the individual is more comfortable. More and more variety in sizing, based on body build as well as body measurements, is being offered on the ready-to-wear market.

Although there is variation in size from one manufacturer to another, it is helpful to know what the various size ranges stand for.

In women's wear, most outer wear clothing sizes are classified as regular Misses, Petite Misses, Womens, Half Sizes and Tall Girl Sizes. Each one is scaled for a different body build. Many underwear manufacturers are adopting a similar size classification.

In men's wear, the chest measurement is important when buying a suit, jacket, sweater or pajamas. The neck measure and sleeve length is needed to determine shirt size. Men's suits range according to body build. They are sized by chest measure in shorts, regulars, and longs. Shorts are for men under 5′ 7″, regulars for men 5′ 7″ to 5′ 11″, and longs for men 5′ 11″ to 6′ 3″.

Manufacturers also designate size in men's garments by body build such as Trim, Stout, and Portly. Men's slacks are sized by waist measure and inseam length and are available in proportioned sizes.

Dress shirts are sized by neck and sleeve measurements, but many sport shirts are classified as small, medium, large or extra large. The size scale most manufacturers use is: small = 14-14½ neck, medium = 15-15½ neck, large = 16-16½ neck and extra large = 17-17½ neck.

Pajamas are given an A, B, C, D size which is scaled to chest measurements. The size scale is: A = Chest 34-36, B = Chest 38-40, C = Chest 42-44, D = Chest 46-48, E = Chest 50-52.

Children's clothing is sized according to weight and height rather than the age of the child.

	BOYS' SIZES					GIRLS' SIZES			
SIZE	HEIGHT	WEIGHT	CHEST	WAIST	SIZE	HEIGHT	WEIGHT	CHEST	WAIST
6	46″	49 lbs.	25″	22½″	7	51″	60 lbs.	26″	22½″
8	50″	59 lbs.	26½″	23½″	8	53″	66 lbs.	27″	23″
10	54″	73 lbs.	28″	24½″	10	55″	74 lbs.	28½″	24″
12	58″	87 lbs.	29½″	25½″	12	57½″	84 lbs.	30″	25″
14	61″	100 lbs.	31½″	26½″	14	60″	96 lbs.	31½″	26″
16	64″	115 lbs.	33″	27½″					
18	66″	126 lbs.	34½″	28½″					

Commercial Standard on Body Measurements developed by the U.S. Dept. of Commerce.

There are some special size ranges for children which may be possible solutions to some of the sizing problem. CHUBBY sizes for girls and HUSKIES for boys may give added room for pelvic bands or body braces and also give a better over-all fit. JUNIOR PETITES and SLIM sizes may be a better fit for children with small bone structures. TALL TEEN fashions are good if added length is necessary but misses sizes would be too large in body measurements.

Too often people are advised to buy larger sizes in clothing to accommodate braces. A larger size may give added room in the area of the braces but it will tend to be too large everywhere else. Clothing that does not fit will not stay in place. Larger sizes provide excessive amounts of fabric which can be uncomfortable to lie on or sit on for long periods of time.

Clothes That Help Prevent Accidents

Careful attention should be given to the safety features of clothing. Certain designs are hazardous and should be avoided such as:

Full loose sleeve styles that can get caught easily;

Dangling ties, belts, scarfs or ornamental buttons;

Loopy fabrics that catch on rough surfaces, furniture or other projecting objects such as door handles or ends of banisters;

Shoes and slippers that have fancy ties or flaps which might cause a person to trip or stumble;

Skirt lengths that catch in the heel of a shoe when a person bends over or climbs stairs.

Clothes That Give Protection and Security

If a person has the added concern of incontinence, the type of protection he uses helps to determine how far he can go from home base with comfort and peace of mind. Since each person has a different problem, it is wise to consult a nurse or some other member of the medical team in order to learn how others have solved this problem. Thousands of incontinent persons have learned to accept and deal with this type of problem and refuse to permit it to limit their activity.

a. Snap front flap style opens flat (Safe-T Pants)
b. Adjustable waistband
c. Adjustable waist and leg bands
d. Flannel snap-in liner for frequent changes
   (Pro-Pants)

Clothing That Will Wear Well

The handicapped person makes greater demands on the wearing qualities of his clothing than is normally expected. For example: When the elbows are used as a lever to help lift the body, there is more wear due to friction. When crutches are used, there is more wear in the underarm section.

Certain characteristic of fabrics and construction contribute to wearability and the more of these that are found, the more insurance there will be that the garment will last longer and wear better.

Fibers, Fabrics and Finishes Contribute to Wearability

Because the wearing qualities of fabrics vary greatly the following guidelines will help individuals make a wise decision in a market of many choices. Wearability of fabric is influenced by the interaction of fiber content, fabric construction, and a wide variety of finishes that can be applied to the fabric.

Although there are many blends of fibers used in fabrics, the textile industry continues to develop new blend combinations to meet special needs and requirements. It is possible to blend fibers so that the qualities of one fiber are enhanced by the qualities of another, thus increasing the desirable characteristics that can be built into a single fabric. For example:

Triacetate helps to make a fabric wrinkle-resistant and gives it stability; that is, it will not shrink or stretch out of shape with normal wear and care.

Polyester gives wrinkle resistance to cotton blend fabrics.

Nylon gives added strength.

Smooth surfaced fabrics made of yarns of the same thickness have more strength than those made with thick and thin yarns. Close, compact woven and knitted fabrics are usually stronger than those of a loose construction.

Permanent finishes give fabrics many desirable qualities and contribute to wearability. For example, finishes are most satisfactory if they guarantee these characteristics: SHRINKAGE CONTROL, WRINKLE RESISTANCE, PERMANENT PRESS, STAIN AND SPOT RESISTANCE, PERSPIRATION RESISTANCE, SOIL RELEASE.

Construction Contributes to Wearability

Strong seams mean sturdy construction and longer-wearing garments. The strength of the seam relates to the strength of the sewing thread, the type of stitch, and the way the seam is finished to keep it from raveling.

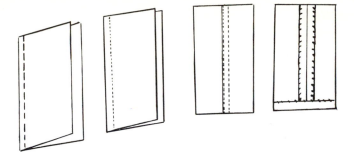

a. Long, loose stitches—weaker seams
b. Small, even stitches—stronger seams
c. Double-stitched seams—stronger seams
d. Overcast seams—stronger seams

Sleeves need to be reinforced by tape or extra rows of stitching along the underarm curve of a kimono sleeve or shoulder line of a raglan sleeve. The tape prevents the stitching from pulling out, when there is strain on the seam, or from stretching out of shape.

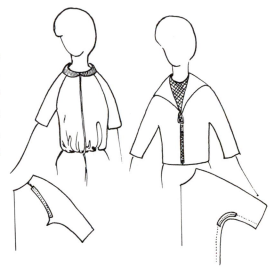

a. Raglan sleeve with tape reinforcement along raglan line
b. Kimono sleeve with tape reinforcement along the underarm curve.

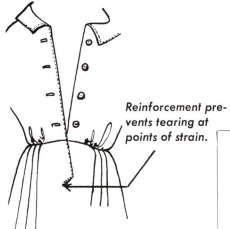

Reinforcement prevents tearing at points of strain.

Openings that end in a seam or those that have been put in by making a slash should be reinforced, since they tear easily.

87

Leather elbow patches are used on sweaters and jackets as a fashion item as well as to give added wear. Other areas may have to be reinforced with double fabrics to take care of the additional wear braces give to clothing.

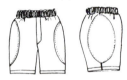

a. Reinforced sides of underpants to prevent brace damage to cloth

b. Reinforced knees of trousers, inside or outside, to prevent brace damage

Clothing That Can Be Cared for Easily

Easy care clothing is of prime importance in saving energy and time. Before buying a garment a person should consider the cost of the upkeep as well as the initial price of the garment. If a garment has to be dry cleaned every time it becomes soiled, it will cost of course more than if it is laundered at home. However, if a person does not have the energy or time to do the laundry at home, the question of whether or not a garment can be dry cleaned is of real importance.

If clothes are bought with easy care in mind, they will look better on the individual both before and after laundering. They will hold their shape better, will wrinkle less and will help a person keep that "well groomed" look.

What Makes Clothing Easy to Care For?

Fabric, design and *construction* determine how easy it will be to care for a garment. All three must be considered to give consumer satisfaction, for if one is overlooked the amount of care will increase.

Since July 3, 1972, apparel manufacturers have been required to attach to all items of wearing apparel (except headwear and footwear) a permanent tag or label that gives care and maintenance instructions for each individual garment. The labels must be accurate, clear, concise and uniform in language. Much of the guesswork has been eliminated from the care of clothing; now it is up to each and every consumer to follow the instructions on the label to achieve satisfactory results.

The common terminology being used on permanent care labels is as follows:

Machine Wash Hot
Machine Wash Separately Hot
Machine Wash Warm
Machine Wash Warm Line Dry
Machine Wash Warm Gentle Tumble Dry Low
Machine Wash Separately Warm
Machine Wash Separately Line Dry
Machine Wash Separately Warm Gentle Tumble Dry Low
Hand Wash Line Dry
Hand Wash Dry Flat
Hand Wash Separately Line Dry
Hand Wash Separately Dry Flat
Dry Clean Only
Wipe With Damp Cloth Only

It is assumed that if a garment is washable it is also dry cleanable.

Additional terms may be added with any of the other terms if they are necessary to communicate what needs to be done with specific garments to assure proper care procedures. Some of these terms[1] are:

Do Not Bleach   Do Not Iron
Do Not Use Chlorine Bleach   Use Cool Iron
Do Not Twist   Furrier Clean Only
Remove Before Fully Dry   Leather Clean Only
Wash Inside Out   Do Not Dry Clean
Wash Separately   Remove Trim

In addition to garments, all piece goods should be sold with a label with care instructions. The consumer is responsible for sewing the label into the garment when it is made.

---

[1] *Guide for Permanent Care Labeling,* prepared by a Joint Retail, Apparel, Textile Industry Committee in Response to the F.T.C. Care Labeling Regulation of December 9, 1971.

CHAPTER 8

Self-Help Clothing
for Women
and for Men

The emphasis on "fashion" as well as "function" in clothes for the handicapped started in the mid-1950's when Dr. Howard A. Rusk, Director of the Institute of Physical Medicine and Rehabilitation in New York City, invited Helen Cookman to head a research project in this area. Mrs. Cookman was selected for two reasons—her years of experience in fashion design and in the manufacturing end of the clothing industry, and her appreciation of the need for clothing that permitted comfort and ease in dressing without sacrificing fashion. She was also very much aware of the psychological need for becoming fashions that would boost the morale of the wearer and add to his or her poise and self-confidence.

The original models were tested on patients at the Institute with the cooperation of Miss Muriel E. Zimmerman, OTR, Associate Chief of Occupational Therapy and Instructor in Physical Medicine and Rehabilitation. The results were published in a very usable manual entitled "Functional Fashions for the Physically Handicapped" (I-6). Some of the models are pictured in this chapter.

As a follow-up on this pilot undertaking, Mrs. Cookman was instrumental in organizing the Clothing Research and Development Foundation, a nonprofit group with a distinguished board of directors headed by Miss Virginia Pope. Recognizing the need for handicapped men and women to feel smartly dressed, this organization contributes to the development of garment design which incorporates special features that make dressing easier for persons with physical limitations. Garments that are approved by the committee assigned to this task are produced by manufacturers selected by the Foundation and distributed throughout the country. Only garments approved by the Clothing Research and Development Foundation may use the label "Functional Fashions".

Cape and *stadium rug* for wheelchair use.

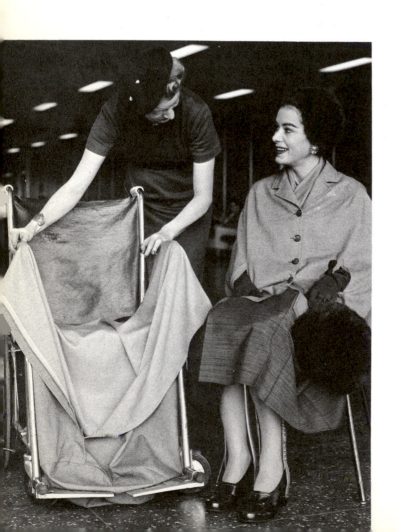

The Clothing and Housing Research Division of the Agriculture Research Service of the U.S.D.A.(H) contributed to the research efforts in this field by developing functional clothing for physically handicapped homemakers. After studying the needs of a group of women with a variety of physical limitations, Clarice Scott (I-7) developed designs which incorporated features considered important for independence as well as ease in accomplishing household tasks.

The bulletin "Clothes for the Physically Handicapped Homemaker" illustrates many of her helpful ideas that could still be used today by the homesewer. Commercial patterns could be adapted to include these features.

Many of the ideas incorporated in these designs take into consideration the movements involved in performing certain household tasks. For example, on one dress the sleeves were designed with an underarm extension of the bodice. This gives the individual added ease for reaching.

The sleeveless blouse, designed for hot weather, is an overblouse style with back pleats close to the armhole for added room.

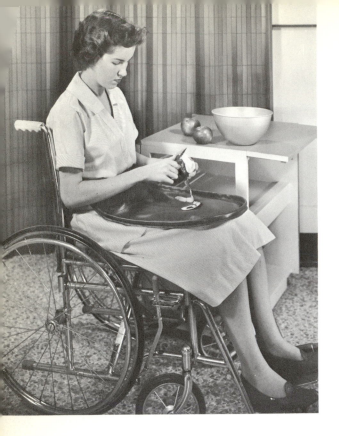

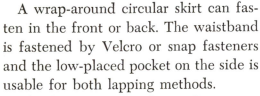

A wrap-around circular skirt can fasten in the front or back. The waistband is fastened by Velcro or snap fasteners and the low-placed pocket on the side is usable for both lapping methods.

The fastener is the design feature on this skirt. The zipper at center front has a fabric tab which makes it easier to open and close.

This apron is made of waterproofed fabric and fits the lap. A plastic clip holds it securely around the waist. It provides a firm work surface and is a protection against hot or cold liquids. Other apron styles supply adequate pockets for transferring articles so that the homemaker's hands may be free to operate her wheelchair.

94

Another group of garments for persons with physical limitations was designed and produced by Mrs. Van Davis Odell. Her mission was to get rid of the frustration involved in fastening undergarments. She developed a mail order business under the label "Fashion-Able" (E) that was primarily concerned with undergarments that fastened with Velcro or zippers. Her early catalogs featured bras with covered Velcro strips instead of hooks and eyes, slips that could be stepped into because of a long zipper-front opening, and girdles that almost completely opened because of four zippers on the front panel.

The growth of this venture has turned "Fashion-Able" into a specialty catalog house that offers outerwear as well as undergarments that make dressing and undressing easier for women of any age. They have also introduced a Shopping Service that offers products of all kinds that would be useful to individuals with limited physical strength or movement.

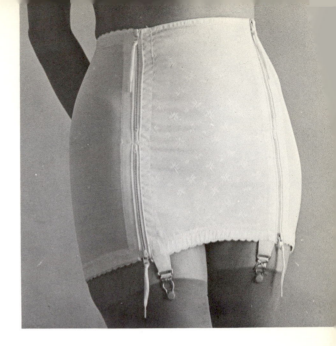

Shop by Mail
Easy-on slacks and blouse with Velcro openings (V.G.R.S.)

The apron with adjustable waistband has terry and plastic-lined "carry-all" pockets (V.G.R.S.).

An agency that has been vitally concerned with helping people to find "attractive, well fitted, and functional clothing" is the Vocational Guidance and Rehabilitation Services (VGRS) of Cleveland, Ohio. VGRS for some time has recognized the importance of special clothing in the rehabilitation process. More than a decade ago, Dorothy A. Behrens (former director of Special Clothing Designs at VGRS) was responsible for the launching of a program which involved the development of new clothing designs as well as the testing and production of garments on a "made to measure" basis.

Today VGRS has an ongoing program, and their catalog which is available for a small fee gives design details and recommends that the customer request swatches of fabrics. It contains several dress styles for the older woman which are available in small, medium, and large sizes. All dresses have either back or front openings with Velcro fastenings. They also have custom slips, both full length and half slip styles. In addition to other garments such as robes, nightgowns, pantsuits, coats, and ponchos, they also carry listings of certain special items of children's wear.

_ *Half-wrap cotton slip with skirt back split at waist (V.G.R.S.)*

Skirt and shorts with adjustable waistbands and Velcro openings (V.G.R.S.)

A Shopper's Guide to Women's Wear

(Compiled from research sources listed in Appendix E and I)

Dress Styles

Dresses with wrap-around style openings or fly-front zipper openings make dressing easier.

Dress styles cut with ease in the bodice area are more practical and comfortable.

Shift styles are good for disguising irregularities. Two-piece dresses allow more freedom for body movement.

Shirt-waist styles are functional if adapted with Velcro under the buttons (D).

Sleeves

Roomy armholes permit ease of movement.

Sleeves should be cut high in the underarm area for the person who uses crutches to avoid distorting the garment and to prevent tearing the fabric.

Short sleeves allow greater freedom for housework and are usually safer than long sleeves.

Necklines

Necklines are a means of calling attention to the face and may help to disguise irregularities. Soft folds that drape around the neck or off-center collars are flattering to most women.

Necklines should not bind or pull back when the individual is seated; they should hug the body.

Slacks or Pants

Slacks slide on over braces better if they are made of woven fabrics rather than knits. Lined pants slow down wear from braces.

Pants with full length side zippers are easier to manage.

Skirts

If skirts are too full they get in the way, and if they are too slim they ride up.

Skirt length should be determined with some awareness of fashion as well as individual needs.

Culottes look like a skirt but give more cover.

98

Jackets, Sweaters, and Coats

Short-length jackets, coats, or capes are more practical than long coats for women in wheelchairs. Since they are less bulky they are more comfortable for the person who sits a great deal.

Car coats are designed for sitting comfort and are easier to put on and take off than a full-length coat.

Coats should be selected to give warmth without weight. The sleeves should not be bulky or cut too deep in the armhole.

Sweaters that are washable are now available in many styles and colors. The special needs of the person who is to wear the garment should be considered before a purchase is made.

Front-Closure and Padded Bras

Stretch bras that go on over the head or are pulled up over the legs and hips require no fastening. Front-closure bras are available but are not easy to find in regular stores. (A brochure on bras and other undergarments designed for persons with physical limitations is available on request from "Fashion-Able" [E].)

A back-closure bra can be made into a front-opening type by inserting Velcro or by using a "bra-refresher" pack (D).

The regular clothing market may offer bras to suit particular requirements: Women who have posture difficulties or involuntary movements will find that bras with stretch straps are comfortable and stay in place. Straps can sometimes be lengthened or shortened and converted to different styles, depending on the neckline of the dress. Straps with a halter adjustment stay in place regardless of body movements.

Padding may be added and bras may be adjusted to fit, if one side of the bust is smaller than the other.

Women who have had a mastectomy may substitute a form to give the figure a balanced appearance so that clothing will fit well. The form can be attached to the bra by snaps to hold it in place, or slipped into a pocket or case made on the inside of the bra. If a slight padding above the bust area is needed, small pads can be purchased, or made, and stitched or snapped into place in either the undergarment or the outer garment, depending on the size of the pad needed.

99

Men's Wear Fashions

One of the greatest innovations for men who wear braces has been the patented Cookman-designed trousers (E). The trousers are made with full-length side-seam zippers. The zippers can be opened all the way from the leg up to the waist or from the waist to the cuff, or they can be zipped half the distance each way. The trousers are also lined in the knee area to protect the pant leg from the wear and tear caused by the knee-locks on braces. Another added feature of the same trousers is a half belt which holds the front or back of the trousers in place during toileting.

The inseam opening suggested for boys' wear and illustrated in (D) can be adapted to men's wear, too. It is a possible solution for men who wear short braces or a prosthesis.

Another "Functional Fashion" is the seat-length suit coat designed for comfort and appearance of men in wheelchairs. It eliminates having to sit on extra fabric that feels bulky and bunches up in wrinkles.

Men who have difficulty with buttons will find Velcro a workable substitution. The buttons can remain on the shirt, but Velcro is positioned behind them, either in a strip or in patches (D). Some men prefer to put their dress shirts on over the head, with most of the buttons prefastened.

Leinenweber, Inc., custom tailors for men's wear, have researched the clothing needs of men in wheelchairs. They have developed a system of tailoring suits and coats to the measurements of men who are constantly sitting. The basis of their designing is to provide comfort by eliminating "material where it isn't needed, and adding it where it helps." (E)

Three features that they claim the individual should look for in a wheelchair suit are:

1. A neat three-button front jacket.
2. A modified coat length to "eliminate 'ride up' in back and discomfort from sitting on coat."
3. Elimination of excess material to remove danger of getting caught in the wheels of the chair.

Trousers are designed so that pockets are more accessible and the seat is cut longer in back for comfortable sitting while the front is shortened.

This mail order house has developed its own system of taking measurements which is explained in detail in a chart that is sent out to the customer with his order blank. They are also willing to incorporate special requests for wear reinforcements or, they will add extra room that might be required by the individual client.

CHAPTER 9

Self-Help Clothing
for Children

Early independence in dressing is desirable for all children. It contributes to the development of initiative, coordination, self-confidence, and a feeling of satisfaction that is sure to be reflected in the behavior of the child. In addition, the child who can dress himself will eventually save his mother an endless amount of energy and time (I-1, 3, 4).

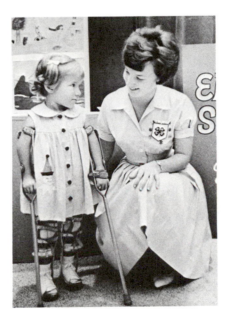

First attempts, which are likely to be undressing rather than dressing, are sure to be clumsy and will take an endless amount of time. This is when parents must give encouragement and be blessed with an enormous amount of patience. The child's success will depend, in part, on whether his clothes are easy for him to handle and whether his parents can restrain themselves from offering help except when it is absolutely needed.

103

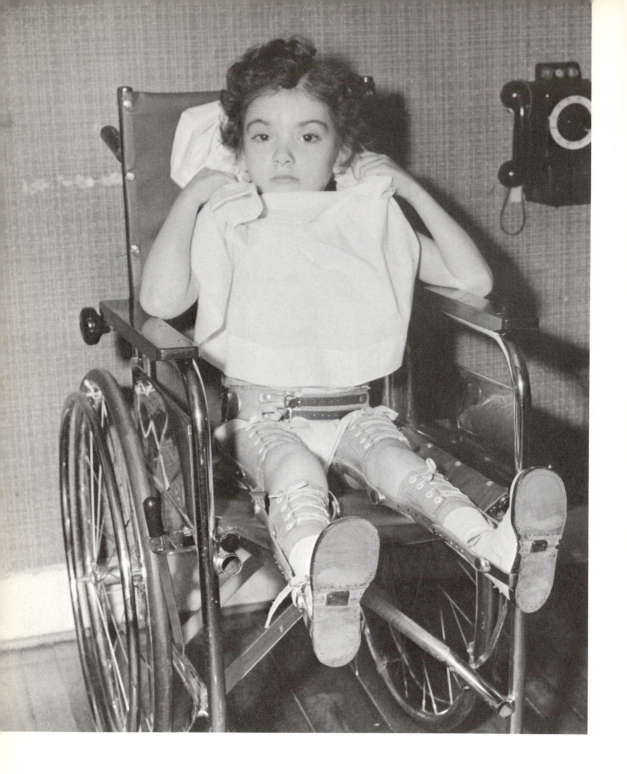

For the first time in her life—she has a dress she can put on by herself.

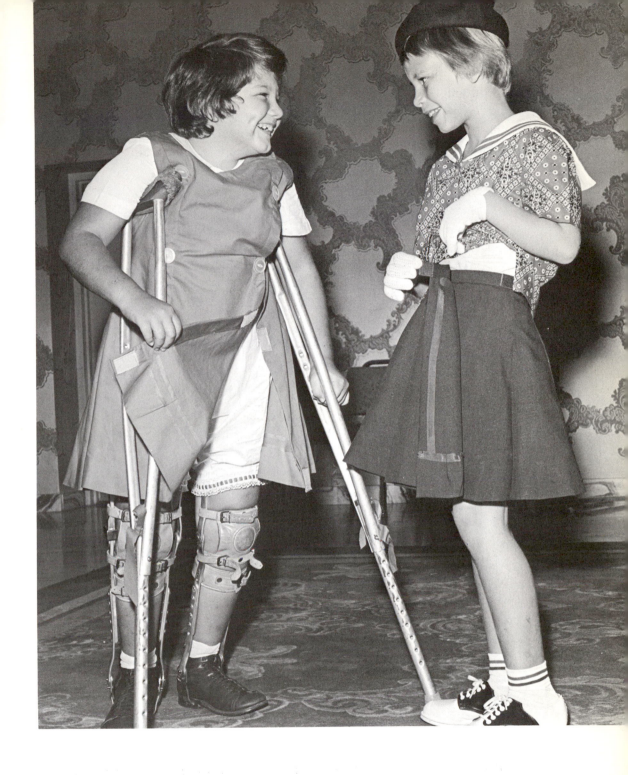

Velcro is used for the front openings of the belt and skirt.

1. Self-Help Clothing

Full-length center-front openings make it possible for children to slip in and out of garments with greater ease. This is particularly true for the child whose body movements are limited. Full-length openings can be found on overalls, coveralls or jumpsuits, dresses, jumpers, shirts, and blouses.

It may be desirable to choose *slip-on styles* with *enlarged neck openings* for some children rather than garments with full-length front openings. This choice will depend on the child's muscle coordination, strength, and range of motion. Children who must sit when dressing may find it easier to slip a garment on over the head. Pajamas and nightgowns can be selected with this design feature as well as dresses, blouses, and shirts.

For the child with limited use of his hands, garments with *expandable neck openings* and *no fasteners* may be more functional. Necklines expand either because the fabric stretches, such as a knitted fabric, or the neckline is designed and cut to give added room when it is pulled on over the head. Some necklines expand because of a shoulder opening; garments of this type go on over the head easily but are more difficult for a child to manage because of the location of the fasteners. Mothers, however, will find this style an added convenience in dressing young children who have not achieved independence.

Expandable neck openings with no fasteners

The *location of the fasteners* is an important factor in helping a child to develop independence in dressing. The best garments are usually those with a center front or side front opening with fasteners that a child can easily reach. Side and back openings are beyond his reach and tend to confuse and discourage the child who is trying to learn how to dress himself. It is desirable to have all of his garments open in a similar way so that a child may learn easily to distinguish front from back. Special markings or a brightly colored tab inserted in the back of the garment can help him decide how to begin to put the garment on.

107

Some children have trouble identifying clothing items because of perceptual difficulties. They may not be able to distinguish the front from the back or the top from the bottom. A little ingenuity may help them achieve success in dressing. Color can be the key to identification. If a child can see color, then blouses and shirts could have dark colors in back and light colors in front or a light top and dark bottom. Such clothing items would probably have to be made, although similar color combinations appear on the market from time to time in children's play clothes.

Dark over light to help identify buttoning direction Dark in back, light in front, helps child to put his garment on correctly.

Garments with no fasteners contribute to ease in dressing for both the handicapped and the non-handicapped child. For this reason the boxer type shorts and slacks are particularly popular with young children.

a. Full boxer style
b. Boxer style with zipper fly and elasticized back waist

Suspender overalls with adjustable straps and elasticized waist

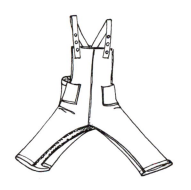

Zipper inserted in crotch seam of overalls.

Young children with protruding abdomens may find it difficult to keep boxer type pants from slipping down. This creates a hazard for any child and especially for those with poor balance or walking difficulties. Suspender pants or overalls are sometimes better choices for young children.

A full-length crotch opening is helpful in caring for young children who are incontinent or who are not completely toilet-trained. Since these openings are found only on infants' and toddlers' overalls, an alteration must be made. The inseam can be opened and a separating jacket zipper inserted into the seam (D).

Knitted separates with elasticized waistbands and rib-knit expandable necklines are practical for children who do not wear braces. (Knitted fabrics cling and catch on brace locks.)

Knits with no fasteners

2. Growth Features

Children grow out of their clothes in a surprisingly short time. Although an outfit may fit when purchased, it is likely to soon become too tight in the crotch, or it may bind in the armhole and become too short in length. The buying of larger sizes than the child needs is not the answer. By the time he grows into a larger size, the garments may be worn out. It is also unsafe to have clothing that is too loose or too baggy, since it may cause accidents. Children in wheelchairs find it uncomfortable to sit on clothing that is too large. For children using crutches it is both annoying and unsafe to have to pull up pants that are big around the waist or shirts that slip off the shoulders.

One solution is to look for clothing designed with growth features, that can be made larger as the child develops. Growth tucks put into a garment with a loose chain stitch can easily be removed to give added length or width. Adjustable shoulder straps and waistbands, kimono and raglan sleeves, all allow for longer wear. Boys' shirts are also being made with expandable collars that actually "grow" up to two sizes. Stretch shirts with stretch collars give this additional room for growth.

a. Vertical growth tucks expand for added shoulder length.
b. Horizontal growth tucks in slip, when released, lower the hem.
c. Adjustable shoulder straps and waistbands

The School-Age Child

When children start school they are likely to insist that their clothing look like that worn by other children. Many of the features which make dressing easier for the young child are more difficult to find in the styles available for the school-age child. Adaptations must be made to provide workable openings and fasteners for children with hand or leg involvements or poor coordination.

Blouses and Skirts

Girls' blouses and boys' shirts usually have small buttons on front openings. These can be adapted for easy fastening by converting the fasteners to Velcro (D). The appearance of the garment remains the same, but it becomes more functional. The children are happy because they can manage Velcro and they do not have to wear clothing that is different than their friends wear.

Dress shirts bring on added problems such as fastening cuffs on long sleeves and wearing ties. Boys with hand limitations will find pre-tied ties that clip on to the shirt collar or hook around the neck are great savers of energy and time. Long sleeves can be fastened at the cuffs with Velcro or an elastic cuff link.

Pre-tied bow and four-in-hand ties

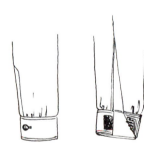

a. *Buttoned cuff*

b. *Velcro replacement*

c. *Elastic thread between two buttons*

d. *Elastic cuff link*

Children who use crutches often have trouble with garments tearing along the underarm seams. Blouses and shirts with double-stitched seams will be more durable. Stretch woven fabric will have more give in this area and will tend to wear longer. A fabric reinforcement, before wear begins, will also help prevent damage.

Sleeveless blouses are comfortable in warm climates, but girls with small frames or underdeveloped bodies will find they are often cut too deep in the armholes. An extra piece of fabric can be inserted under the arm to raise the armhole (D).

Long sleeves are troublesome for children in wheelchairs since the sleeves have a tendency to pick up dirt from the wheels.

Overblouse styles are good for disguising figure irregularities. They also give added room for body movement and are usually easy styles to put on. Many boys' shirts are designed to be worn outside the trousers and are a good cover-up for body irregularities.

Skirts and Culottes

Girls with involvements in the lower extremities need skirts with some flare, but excessive fullness is cumbersome. The girl who walks with a forward body movement may have the problem of extra fullness all hanging in the front. Girls in wheelchairs find extra fullness an added nuisance, since the skirt has to be arranged carefully in the chair so that it will not get caught in the wheels. They also dislike skirts that are longer than those worn by their contemporaries.

Wrap-around skirt styles and culottes

Slim straight skirts are not very practical because they have a tendency to ride up. They also do not allow much room for leg movement when transferring from a wheelchair. Wrap-around style skirts are convenient for toileting and are easy to put on. Culottes look like skirts but are actually pants. They are comfortable and allow more room for body movement without the worry or embarrassment of exposure. Culottes give ample room for braces and lend themselves to the swinging movement of the girl who uses crutches.

Center front openings are usually more convenient than side openings. If side openings are used, they should be on the side opposite the stronger hand. Elasticized or adjustable waistbands are practical for girls who wear braces or those with fluctuating waistlines.

a. Elasticized waistbands
b. Snap adjustable waistbands
c. Button adjustable waistbands

113

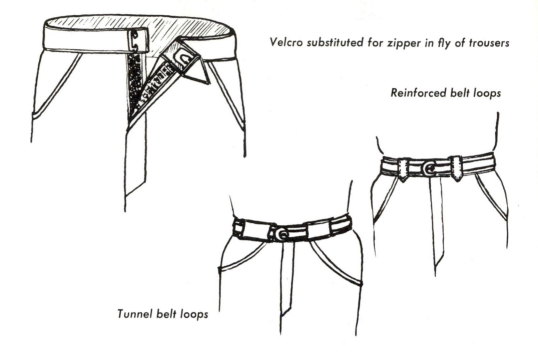

Velcro substituted for zipper in fly of trousers

Reinforced belt loops

Tunnel belt loops

Slacks, Overalls, Shorts

One of the major problems boys face in dressing is the tapered slim legs found on some trousers. The slim legs make it impossible to slip the trousers on over leg braces. The most workable solution is to open the inseam of the trouser leg and insert a zipper or Velcro into the seam (D). The length of the opening should relate to the length of the braces.

Another problem boys have with trousers is that of locking the zipper at the top of the fly. Velcro seems to be a good substitute for zippers in the fly front, particularly for those who have some hand involvement or poor coordination—Velcro is easy to manage and a pat closes the fly securely. A large hook closure at the waist is more secure and easier to fasten than a snap or button.

Boys who are unable to walk may face the problem of being lifted from their wheelchairs to cars or other areas. It helps the person doing the lifting if he can grasp the belt or belt loops of the boy's trousers. To make this workable, the trousers must fit well around the waist and the belt loops must be strong, like tunnel loops, or else be reinforced.

Girls with leg braces have much the same problem as boys in getting into tapered pants. Straight cut pants or flares have more room in the leg area and may not require any adaptation. Full cut styles are made for boys, too, but some do not accept them. However, just as fashions change, so do attitudes; what is not accepted today may be popular tomorrow! Bermuda shorts are good all-year-round wear for children with leg braces. Worn with knee socks, they look smart and add to the ease of dressing. Since they are available in woolen fabrics as well as cotton, they are suitable for different climates and seasons of the year. Shorts and pants may be worn to school depending on the school and the attitude of other children.

Dresses

The ideal style for most girls with physical limitations is the shift or one-piece dress with no waistline seam. It is adaptable to many different figures, helps to camouflage figure irregularities, and fits over braces.

Shift Styles
Dress styles suitable for disguising and adjusting to figure irregularities

Two-Piece Fashions
Two-piece dress styles adjust to body irregularities better than one-piece styles.

The hem line on a two-piece dress is not affected by a low shoulder.

Teen-age girls with an upper extremity prosthesis often have difficulty in finding dresses with long sleeves. It may be possible to have dresses made or perhaps the store where the dress is purchased can order extra fabric to match the dress so that sleeves may be added without spoiling the design.

A smart girl will play up her weak points to her advantage, through wise clothing selection. This is one way of achieving individuality. For example, if a girl must wear high necks, consider dramatizing this feature with a becoming color or draped folds, to gain interest.

It is easier to have an attractive and neat appearance if the hemline of a garment appears to be balanced. An uneven hemline can be caused by poor posture, some body irregularity or by an uneven walking gait. The hem should be adjusted carefully to suit the way the child stands or walks. Girls who are small in stature and have an irregularity in the back or shoulder area may find two-piece dresses fit and hang better on their figures. The hemline of the skirt is then not affected by any irregularity in the upper part of the body.

Sweaters, Jackets, and Coats

Cardigan-style sweaters are easy to put on and take off. Some styles have zipper closures. Velcro may be substituted for the buttons.

Lightweight jackets that are warm without being heavy or bulky are now available. Foam laminates, a foam backing applied to another fabric, and nylon quilted to polyester fiberfill provide insulation from cold temperatures and wind but are light in weight for freedom of movement.

Children with poor muscle coordination or hand involvements may find it difficult to fit a zipper together at the bottom of the jacket before it is zipped up. A Velcro closing on the jacket may be easier to manage (D). A large snap, placed at the bottom of the front opening of the jacket, helps to line up the Velcro.

Jackets and coats should be roomy in cut to meet the needs of children with involuntary movements, weak muscles, limited shoulder movement or with artificial arms or hands. Sleeves should be large enough in the armhole for ease in dressing but not too bulky or too deep in cut. A full-length crutch should fit comfortably under the arm without changing the line of the dress. The arm cuffs on a Canadian or Loftstand crutch should fit over coat sleeves.

Easy-to-wear Outdoor Garments
Self-help jacket and cape styles

Footwear: Shoes, Boots, and Slippers

Shoes present one of the most difficult dressing problems for a child because lacing and tying demand fine motor coordination. Some other means of fastening should be considered such as the "Shu-lok" fastener which flips up to open and snaps closed over the instep. Shoe styles with snap-lock straps or straps that fasten with Velcro, are easy to manage. A shoe repairman can stitch strips of Velcro to a strap shoe in place of buckles.

Some children need corrective shoes for additional support or to improve body posture and balance. If lacing is difficult the method of solving this problem must be adapted to the individual child. Occupational therapists can often suggest ingenious solutions for individual problems.

When zippers are used to replace laces, the repairman should extend the length of the opening so there is adequate room to get in and out of the shoes easily. Elastic shoe laces are another possible solution to the problem. Children with flail or spastic feet may need shoes that open all the way to the toes. The shoe can be opened and the lacing eyelets extended.

When a child is paralyzed in the lower extremities, shoe styles that allow for some swelling of the feet are a good choice. Slip-on styles like moccasins do not cramp the feet but children in wheel chairs may find they need straps to keep such shoes on their feet.

Slippers are easy to slip on and off but children may have difficulty in keeping them on their feet. High slippers with zipper openings or elastic loops or button fasteners are easy to get into and are more likely to stay on restless feet.

Boots and overshoes must be large enough to slip on easily over shoes. The length and the location of the opening are the important features to look for.

Socks and Stockings

Socks tend to stretch out of shape from excessive pulling and then slip down over the heel or slide into the shoe when they are worn. Elastic tops hold their shape but are not easy to pull on and they may interfere with circulation. Stretch socks keep their shape but are sometimes more difficult to pull on depending on the amount of stretch that is built into the sock either through the fiber content or the construction. Reinforcements in the heel area will improve wearing quality.

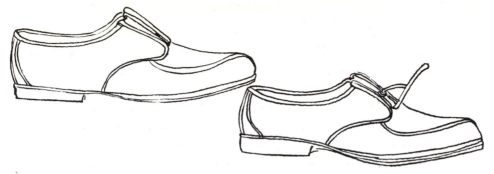

Shu-Lok fasteners

Slipper styles that stay on the feet

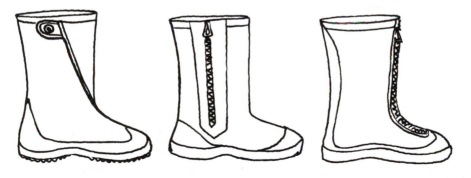

Boot styles with openings and fasteners for easy dressing

Underwear

Undershirts and underpants that fit properly, will require the same care and consideration of the child's needs in selection as that taken in choosing his outerwear. Children in wheelchairs need underwear that does not creep up or get wrinkled as they sit. Children with braces need underwear with allowances in cut to give adequate room. Their underwear should also be reinforced in areas that involve friction. Some manufacturers use nylon to reinforce cotton undershirts and pants, to give added strength. If the underwear has not been reinforced, it is wise to make this adjustment before there are signs of wear.

Underpants and shirt styles for girls.
a. Brief and longer length
b. Pettipants
c. Vest-type shirt and expandable neck shirt

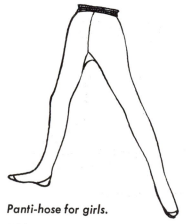

Panti-hose for girls.

For girls, opaque tights and panty hose are available in "one size fits all" or in proportioned sizes according to weight and height measurements.

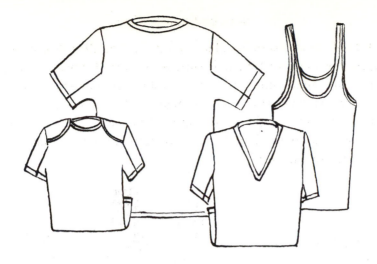

Undershirt styles for boys.
a. *Expandable neck with action sleeves*
b. *Crew neck with action sleeves*
c. *V-neck with action sleeves*
d. *Athletic style*

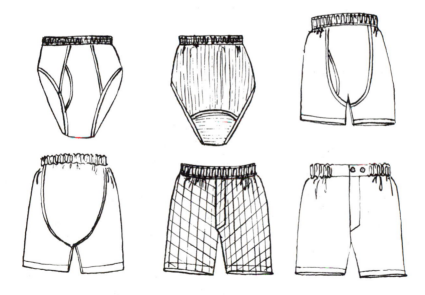

Underpants styles for boys.
a. *Briefs—no-seam seat*
b. *Mid-length shorts—contour seat*
c. *Boxer shorts—full style and fly-front opening*

Slips and Blouse Slips

The style of the slip should relate to a girl's disability. For example: Girls wearing braces will find that half slips have more fullness through the hip area than a full-length slip. Girls with involuntary movements will find slips with broader shoulder straps stay in place better than narrow straps. Slips may not be necessary if the outer garment is lined. If girls in wheelchairs are self-conscious about their body development, a camisole top may suit their needs better than a full slip.

Slip Styles
a. *Half slip*
b. *Slip with adjustable waist*
c. *"Grow" slip—growth tuck at waist*
d. *Elasticized side panel*

Blouse slip and sweater slip

For younger children, slips with elasticized back or side panels give a better fit and added room for movement. These slips, however, usually have fitted waistline seams which tend to interfere with pelvic bands or body braces. In this case straight slips with built-up shoulder straps would be a better choice.

Blouse slips and sweater slips are handy in that they combine two garments in one. They also eliminate the shirttail problems of blouses pulling out of the waistband of a skirt.

122

CHAPTER 10

Devices, Tools,
and Techniques
That Save Energy and Time

Tools and assistive devices cannot take the place of good home management practices but they may make all the difference between success or failure in mastering a particular job.

Since disabilities vary, gadgets are necessarily highly individual. The most functional are often those developed by the handicapped person himself, or by his family, or by occupational therapists.

Basic Considerations in the Selection of Devices

Use ordinary tools when they can be managed. Many homemakers hesitate to use tools that are obviously designed for the handicapped.

Homemakers are more likely to use the assistive devices if they have a part in their selection.

Choose simple tools and, before purchasing, consider the complications involved in taking them apart, keeping them clean, and finding a place to store them.

Consider an assistive device as temporary if that is possible. Change it as the homemaker acquires new skills.

Homemakers with Hand Limitations

Homemakers with hand limitations have the problem of finding suitable tools or of developing skills to compensate. Although a manufacturer may describe a tool as "one-handed," its usefulness will depend on the strength or grasp of the person using it.

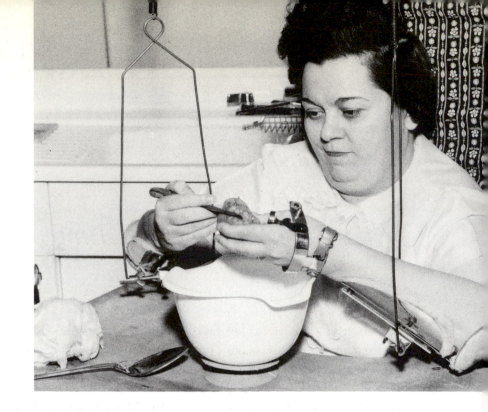

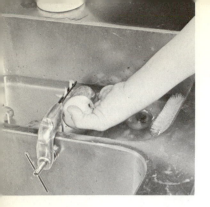
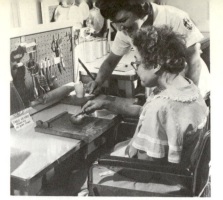

Stabilizing and Holding Devices

Mount containers when possible—such as foil, waxed paper, towels, paper napkins, etc.

The method used in peeling fruits and vegetables with one hand will depend on the homemaker's finger dexterity. The peeler may be stabilized, the item to be peeled may be fastened on an aluminum spike on a board (I-49), or a damp sponge may serve as a stabilizing base. In any case, sharp knives are necessary.

Lightweight bowls may be stabilized by placing them on a damp cloth or double suction cup (G-9) or by holes cut into a pull-out board or a board fitted over a drawer.

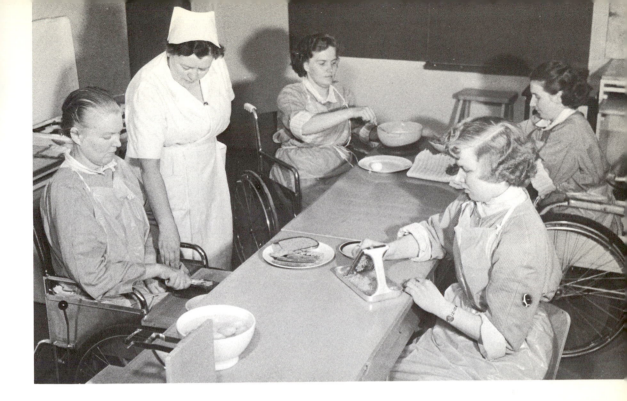

In Finland, training in food preparation for both men and women is often started in the hospital or rehabilitation center. It is also part of the regular program for children in the hospital school. Patients are taught the use of devices and short cuts in meal management.

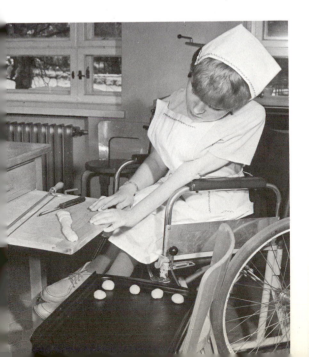

Devices for Those with Problems of Balance

Support of the ordinary window washer's safety strap enables this young person to work with confidence. Standing is part of her therapy program.

Using parallel bars for support while hanging clothes is another opportunity for standing therapy.

Grab bars can be added to the kitchen sink. Note the brushes stabilized with suction cups to help in washing dishes, and the device for turning on faucets (I-49).

A grab bar near the cooking area adds to the convenience and safety of this kitchen (G-9, 11, 12, 29, 33).

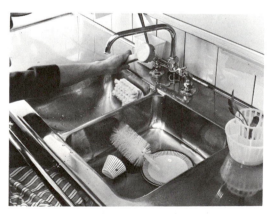

Devices to Simplify Food Preparation

Selection of Utensils

Select utensils which require a minimum of care.

Select easy-to-grasp handles for pans, measuring cups, ladles.

Cooking utensils and measuring spoons should have flat bottoms so they will not tip when set on the counter. Be sure the holes or rings by which they should be hung do not require too fine finger coordination.

Many utensils can be made more useful by enlarging or lengthening handles or by adding holding devices to stabilize them (I-49).

Larger knobs or handles can be substituted on tops of canisters and pan lids, if grasping is a problem.

Strainer lids make it possible to drain off hot liquids safely. Perforated spoons or ladles will also help in lifting out contents from hot liquids.

Tools for Food Preparation

Tools to Simplify Food Preparation

A chef's knife used with a rocker motion works very well for chopping vegetables (G-5, 7). An old-fashioned curved blade chopping device and a wooden bowl are easy to manage (G-6, 8). An electric knife may do the job with seemingly little effort, but it may be impossible for the homemaker to insert and remove blades (G-6,8).

There are several commercial egg separators on the market, but a simple funnel will work just as well (G-6, 8).

A single container which measures and pours is an advantage in food preparation. (The lines can be made with liquid nail polish.) Note easy-to-grasp handle and the cover to help in avoiding accidents (G-6).

A device for pouring liquids for the use of those with involuntary movements can be made by mounting a box on ball bearings, between two uprights. The box swings free and is easy to control.

Electrical appliances such as cooking units, range tops, fry pans, griddles, percolators, may be safer than a stove of conventional height for the homemaker in a wheelchair, if they are placed on a working surface of a comfortable height.

Small equipment is used in teaching nutrition through meal preparation. Patients plan lunches and divide up preparation responsibilities.

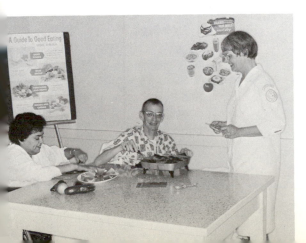

Tools for the Mixing Center

Tools for mixing and beating present special problems. Electric models may be easy to use but difficult to assemble. The one-handed beaters require rather strong pressure but can be used with two weak hands. A whisk may take longer but is quite simple to use and wash (G-6-8).

The problem of safety is a concern for all home-makers. Those with physical limitations must exercise special care. The slotted spoon for lifting vegetables eliminates the necessity of pouring off hot water (G-6-8).

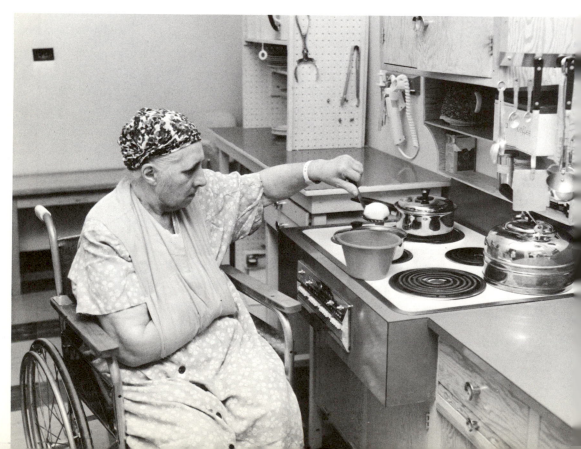

Tools to Simplify Baking

Rolling pastry with one hand may be done with a conventional rolling pin by using the hand directly, or the rolling pin may be fitted with a single handle of wire or wood (I-49). A paint roller may also be used, since it is designed to be used with one hand (G-5).

By folding them into quarters, pastries can be picked up with one hand.

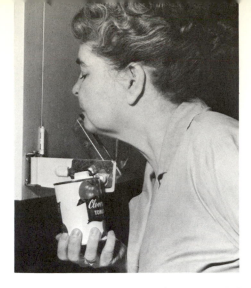

This commercial model is practical for many limited to the use of one hand (G-23).

A conventional opener can be operated if the chin is used, in place of the missing hand, to position cutting lever.

Devices for Opening Cans and Bottles

Many homemakers with hand limitations find the small manual can openers difficult to operate because they cannot hold the can or grasp the turning device or because they do not have the strength necessary to turn it.

Electric openers may prove helpful to some but for others the piercing lever requires too much strength, or the releasing mechanism may be difficult to manage, or they may have no way to hold the can. These features should be checked before a purchase is made.

Canned milk companies suggest a two-prong punch opener for opening evaporated or condensed milk cans. Strong pressure is required. Wall-mounted wedge openers are helpful in opening screw-type jars (I-42, 45). Wall-mounted bottle openers remove caps easily (I-42, 45).

The hinged side of a door may serve as a vise to hold bottle caps on syrup, catsup, etc., while the homemaker turns the bottle. Larger jars can be held securely between the knees or wedged in a drawer.

Devices to Make Dishwashing Easier

Electric dishwashers save a great deal of labor, but the initial cost is high. Various dishwashing devices (G-16) may be attached to the faucets, but most people continue to do them by hand.

Sink racks help raise the dishpan to a more convenient height in a deep sink. (I-45, G-32).

Brushes or dish mops stabilized with suction cups are useful (I-49).

A rubber drainboard will provide an easy-to-clean work surface (G-8, 32).

A rubber sink liner or mat will reduce breakage (G-8, 32).

Plastic-coated racks for air drying of dishes save time and energy (G-6, 8, 32).

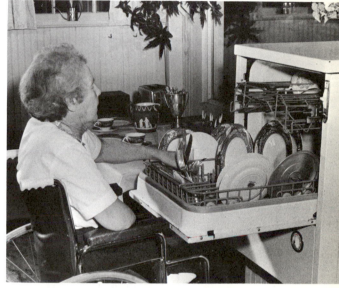

A dining area has been arranged in front of a picture window in the kitchen. The table is on casters so it can be moved to the sink for rinsing dishes. The dishwasher was raised to the level of the table for convenience in loading and unloading.

135

attached to a rail contrivance in the ceiling, for weak or paralysed arms.

type with diagonal inter-balance.

Grater for the one-armed housewife.

Coffee pot for the blind.

Tap open

Cupboard with sliding shelves. Cupboard door equipped with magnetic lock.

Knee-space under sink.

Flooring of lino and plastic.

Wheel-chair adjustable in height.

Potato peelers for t one-armed housewi

The Rehabilitation Bus which has traveled all over Sweden is equipped with many helpful devices for the homemaker with physical limitations. A similar program is now in progress in Nebraska, directed by the College of Home Economics of the University.

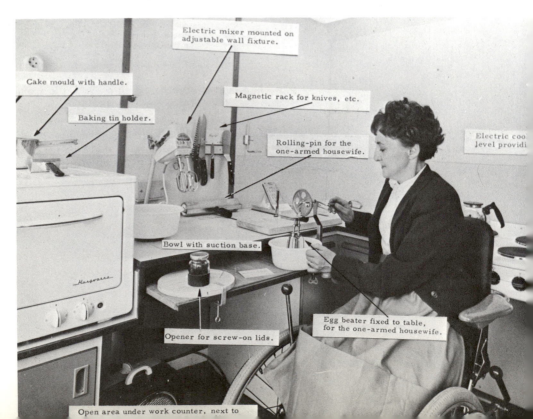

Electric mixer mounted on adjustable wall fixture.

Cake mould with handle.

Magnetic rack for knives, etc.

Baking tin holder.

Rolling-pin for the one-armed housewife.

Electric coo level providi

Bowl with suction base.

Opener for screw-on lids.

Egg beater fixed to table, for the one-armed housewife.

Open area under work counter, next to

Devices to Make Cleaning Easier

For the homemaker in a wheelchair, short handles are easier to handle. This is a child's lightweight mop.

Short-handled tools are easier to control with a prosthesis.

A vacuum without wheels can be transported when attached to the back of a chair. Those with wheels can be moved along with the chair. Some homemakers prefer an electric broom because of the light weight. A carpet sweeper is easily managed (G-6-8).

No lifting or carrying is required when equipment is placed on wheels (G-14, 18).

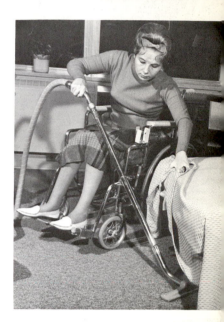

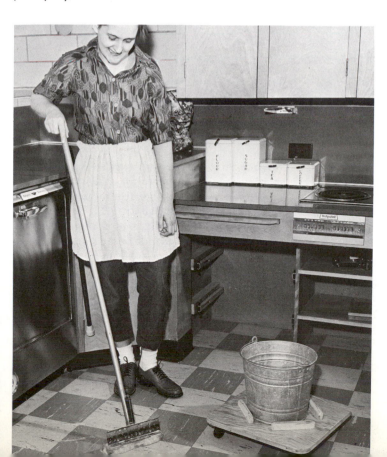

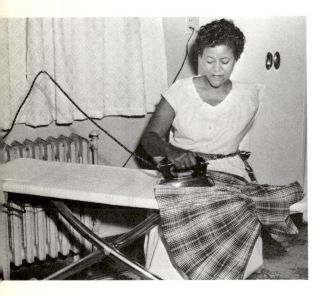

Tools for Doing the Laundry

Racks which can be raised or lowered over the bathtub simplify the drying of clothes indoors (G-6).

An adjustable board on wheels and a cord minder make it possible for this homemaker limited to the use of one hand to set up her own equipment and do her ironing (G-6-8). A "left-handed" iron, or one with the cord attached to the center back rather than to the side, is a distinct advantage for a person who irons with the left hand (G-35).

The iron may be guided with the forearm while the fingers smooth the garment ahead of the iron.

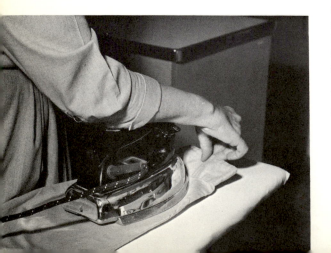

 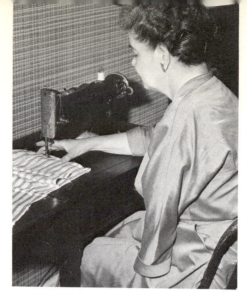

Devices for Sewing

A prosthesis makes a useful holding device for embroidery or sewing.

The large flat surface to the left helps in holding the material which is guided under the needle with the fingers of one hand rather than by the usual two-handed method.

This sewing center is designed with a table surface which can be used for cutting out garments, for stitching by machine, for pressing seams, or for hand sewing, and also for writing and a variety of other activities. Storage areas are provided for the sewing machine, sewing supplies, an iron, and small ironing board. An electric raising mechanism adjusts to heights for use while standing or sitting in a chair. When it is slipped over the end of a single bed, it provides an excellent work surface. A crank mechanism, such as used on a hospital bed, may be substituted for the electric motor to operate the elevating device (I-51).

A cantilevered sewing and ironing unit designed for the 1962 London Exhibition: "Toward Housing the Disabled."

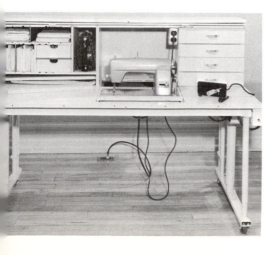 

Devices for Sewing, Mending, and Hand Work

Darning, hemming, knitting, and crocheting can be managed with one hand by using a clamp device to hold either the fabric or the tool.

Plenty of pins, a flat surface and the weight of pinking shears hold the fabric pieces for basting with one hand. For threading needles, some homemakers depend on the commercial "needle threader" (G-6-7). Left-handed scissors simplify the cutting process for the person limited to the use of the left hand (G-17). Electric scissors are also worth considering (G-8).

When a homemaker is limited to the use of one hand, she must acquire skill in finger manipulation. A bit of Scotch tape will hold the button in position for sewing.

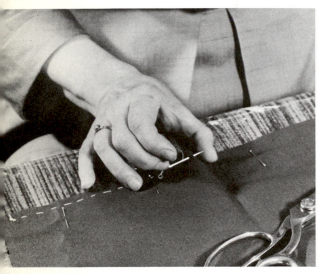

Devices for Extending Reach

Long-handled and short-handled pick-up devices are many and varied. Some are made of wood, some of aluminum

or other metals. Some are tipped with magnets, or hooks, or clamps, or simple rubber devices (G-8, 17, 18, 25, E-4).

To save steps, a duplicate set of tongs may be hung at various work centers or an extra set may be carried in a wheelchair.

Extension handles have been added to brushes, window washing devices, dusters, and scrubbers for the bathtub to eliminate stooping or reaching (G-14, 17, 19, 33).

Conventional storage cupboards with stationary shelves can be made more useful by adding homemade or commercial half-shelves, turntables—with or without storage bins—and devices such as storage shelves and pan and lid racks. Nylon glides insure ease in operation (G-8, 32).

Small items may be hung within easy reach by using bar magnets, suction cup hooks, magnetized hooks, slots, peg board, etc. (G-6, 8, 14, 17). Small storage devices such as spice racks may be put on the inside of cupboard doors.

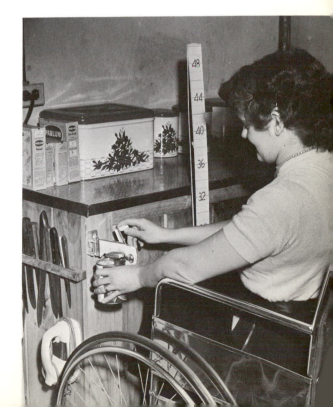

Trays, Carts, and Chairs

Wheelchair trays should be easy to attach and well anchored. The size and shape selected will depend on the type of chair and also on the intended use (I-49), (G-9, 13).

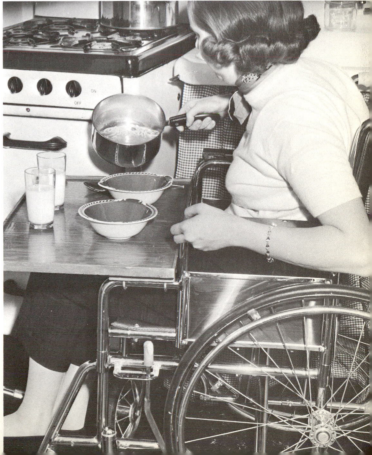

A tray that can be adjusted in height can serve several purposes. (Notice that the balcony of this home is on the same floor level as the living room and that the window-door is wide enough for easy access with a wheelchair.)

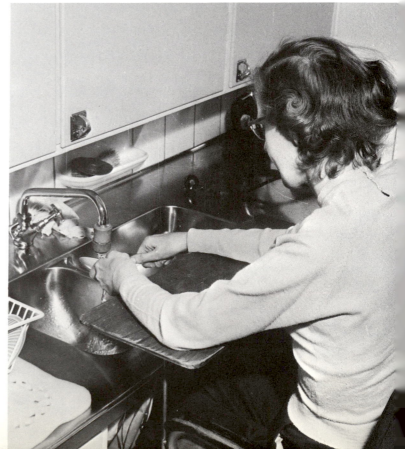

A larger lap tray may serve as a good working surface for dressing a child or for food preparation.

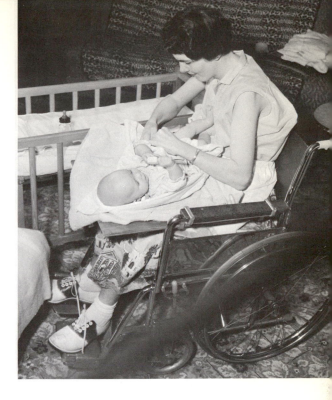

A waist-high tea cart is useful as a support for walking and also for transporting.

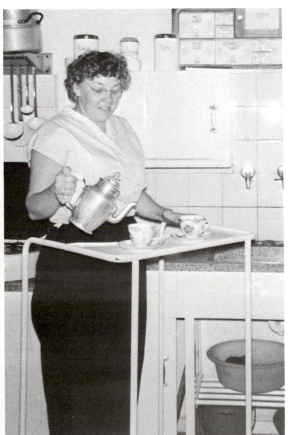

A sturdy cart furnishes support for this homemaker with cerebral palsy.

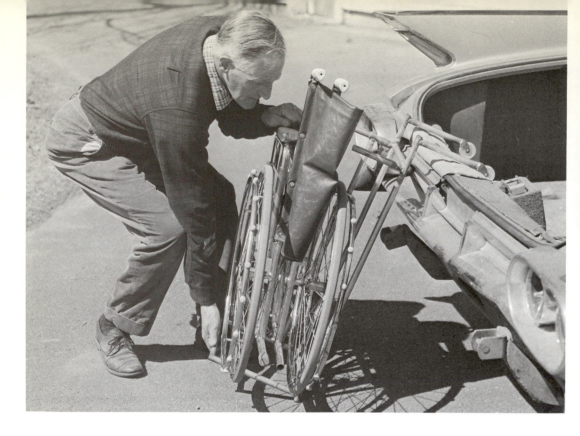

Device for Lifting Wheelchair

A simple device can assist in lifting a wheelchair into the trunk of the car. (See Appendix B for drawings.)

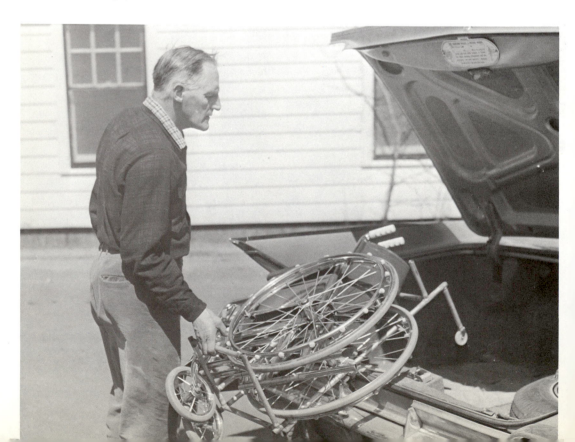

A Trailer for a Wheelchair

This battery-powered chair can be easily loaded into a small trailer and attached to any car. (Made by Tony Markland, Storrs, Connecticut.)

This homemade padded wedge may be slipped into the space next to the car seat to permit an easier transfer from the wheelchair to the car. Bars over the door-window and front window enable this homemaker to get into the car with very little help. The chair is for indoor use and does not fold.

This narrow chair, designed by the owner, has been used in international travel tours. It is well adapted to indoor use and convenient for housekeeping chores.

The hydraulic wheelchair is convenient for reaching high places.

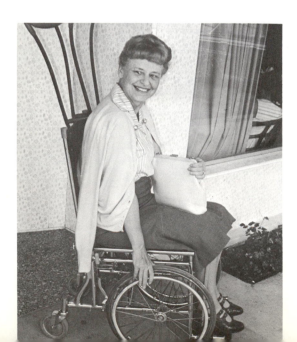 

 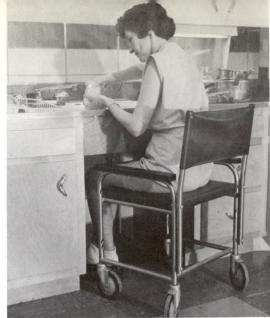

Smaller chairs with wheels may replace the wheelchair in the house if the homemaker can push with her feet.

An inexpensive "sit-to-work" chair can be made at home. This involves putting an ordinary chair on a dolly with good ball bearing casters. The legs should be cut off so the home-maker can rest her feet flat on the floor or operate easily with her feet (B).

This outdoor gasoline-powered chair was designed and constructed by a local garage from parts of seventeen different machines, including a lawn mower, vacuum cleaner, truck, motor scooter, and various automobiles. It will travel over lawns and even along woodland paths. (Made by Tony Markland, Storrs, Connecticut.)

Simple Elevators and Stair Climber

This young woman travels to her office in a car which has been adapted to suit her particular needs. She has solved the stair-climbing problem by installing a hydraulic lift that takes her from her garage to the level of her kitchen door (G-27, I-25 and 40).

A balsa wood block with non-skid rubber caps fastened to the end of a cane not only gives the user a firm handhold but reduces the height of the riser by half.

151

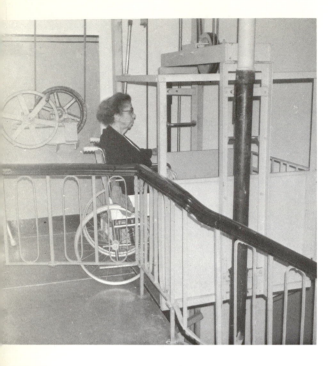
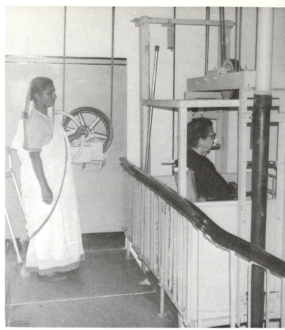

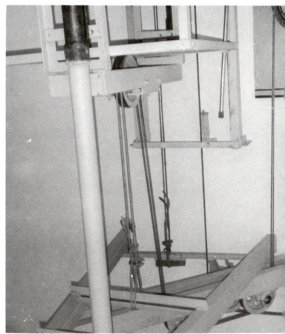

This hand-operated elevator was constructed in the stairwell of a home with very high ceilings in New Delhi.

CHAPTER 11

Housing and Kitchen Planning for the Handicapped and the Elderly

Some Examples of Research, Demonstration, and Training

Research and demonstrations in housing and homemaking activities make it possible for persons, who might have been labeled "shut-ins," to become relatively independent. This is due to the removal of architectural barriers (I-23-26), the adaptation of household equipment, the development of transportation facilities to suit the needs of handicapped persons (I-25), the opportunities now offered for training for independence, both in the home and outside of the home, and the inspiration of those who have achieved a degree of independence in spite of physical limitations.

Trends in Housing for the Physically Limited

Segregated housing for older people and people with physical limitations, was once the accepted pattern. The trend now, particularly in·Europe, is to make it possible for the handicapped and aging to live in developments which also include the non-handicapped in all age groups. Certain apartments have wide doorways for wheelchairs, non-skid floor finishes, lighting facilities within easy reach, bathrooms with grab bars for safety and facilities placed at a comfortable height, and kitchen equipment arranged for the comfort, convenience, and safety.

Many apartments have balconies for hobby interests such as flower box gardens and bird feeding stations. Elevators take handicapped persons directly to the basement where they may use a ramp to go to the street or get into a car.

International concern over housing for the handicapped is reflected in new research, new publications, and new legislation to extend public housing programs to include handicapped persons.

In Sweden, seven hundred "invalid flats" have been developed in old houses and in new housing units. The long-time plan is to enable as many persons as possible to live at home with their families. State subsidy and homemakers' insurance policies help to finance the program (I-106).

In some cities in The Netherlands there are "health houses," designed for maximum independence of handicapped persons. Doorways are designed to enable persons to enjoy balconies or small gardens. The assignment of houses is under the direction of the Municipal Medical Health Services. One of the research reports is printed in English and is available in the United States. This photograph of the model of the wheelchair house appears in the publication (I-34).

In Great Britain a nation wide program on housing for the handicapped is in progress. A new manual published by the Institute of British Architects is an excellent source of information on standards for housing to suit various disabilities (I-26).

In the United States, federal concern for housing for the handicapped, which began with legislation for housing for handicapped veterans, now includes provision for single handicapped persons in municipal housing projects as well as for handicapped persons living with their families. Details on the Housing Act of 1964 are available through local housing authorities or from the Federal Housing Administration (H). Resource material on housing for the handicapped is also available from such agencies as: The U.S. Department of Agriculture (H); The American Standards Association (H); The Small Homes Council (H); The National Society for Crippled Children and Adults (H); The Housing Research Center of Cornell (H); and the National Council on Aging (H).

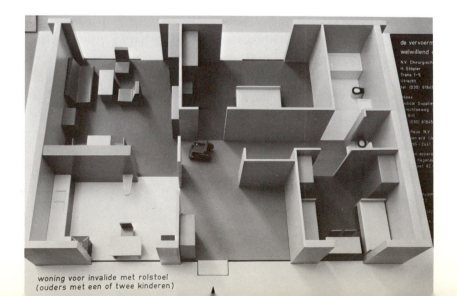

woning voor invalide met rolstoel
(ouders met een of twee kinderen)

The "Functional Home for Easier Living," a demonstration house located in the heart of New York City adjoining the Institute of Physical Medicine and Rehabilitation, is an example of housing for persons with physical limitations. It is used as a training center for patients in the Institute and is visited every year by thousands of people from all parts of the world (I-37).

The furniture was selected for the comfort and convenience of persons with physical limitations. Chairs and couches have firm cushions and arms to serve as a support for rising or sitting. The height of the seats has been raised by extending the legs (I-24).

Some Special Features of a Home Built for a Mother Confined to a Wheelchair

There are advantages, of course, in having a house built to suit a particular person. The series of pictures which follows shows results of such planning by a young mother confined to a wheelchair.

The entrance has a low threshold and a walk with just enough slope to drain easily. The roof overhang protects the entrance in winter from icy drips. The level of the floor leading to the screened porch is the same as the inside floor.

Easy-to-reach casement-type windows and screens made as a unit, can be controlled from the inside (G-4).

Chests and storage cupboards can be built in to eliminate cleaning underneath and also to save space. For this same reason, shelves and bookcases may be either wall-hung or built to the floor.

Cleaning is simplified by a built-in vacuum system with a tank in the basement that need not be emptied more than once in two or three months (G-8, 22). The wall outlets are located at a convenient height in several positions in the house. The only parts that require moving are a flexible hose and various lightweight cleaning attachments.

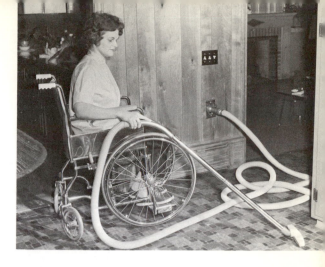

The kitchen has a number of time- and energy-saving features.

Comfortable working heights and continuous counters to permit the sliding of utensils and to minimize lifting.

The sink allows room for the arms of the wheelchair.

The door of the front-opening dishwasher adjoins the Lazy Susan for storing dishes. This is convenient for this homemaker, since she has strong arms and good sitting balance.

Some Special Features of a House Built for an Unusually Tall Homemaker with Problems of Balance, Bending, and Lifting

The corner of the cabinets and the door to the mixer make a three-sided support. All supplies and equipment are within easy reach.

Gravity bins for flour and sugar reduce lifting. File storage makes pans easy to grasp. Counters have been raised from the standard 36-inch height to 40 inches.

Wall plugs were installed at 26 inches from the floor to minimize bending.

To minimize bending, the bathtub was installed at 12 inches from the floor. The broad brim and raised height enabled her to sit on the side and swing her feet over into the tub.

This lavatory vanity counter, extended in length and installed at a 40-inch height, makes a comfortable working height for dressing and bathing the baby.

The bed has been raised to 30 inches from the floor in order to minimize bending to make the bed and to facilitate getting in and out of bed. Built-in storage drawers underneath the bed utilize waste space and eliminate the need for cleaning under the bed. The storage drawers are for extra blankets and little-used items, since they must be operated by the non-handicapped members of the family.

A well-constructed ramp leads directly to the driveway beside the house. (Specifications for ramps to suit particular disabilities are available through the National Society for Crippled Children and Adults.) (1-23, 25, 30)

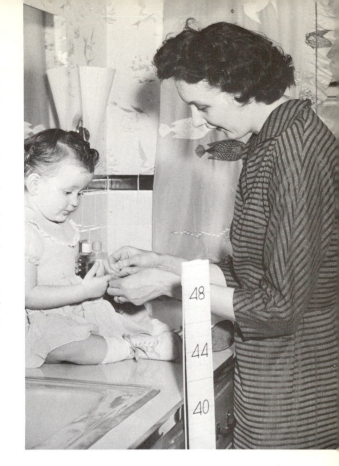

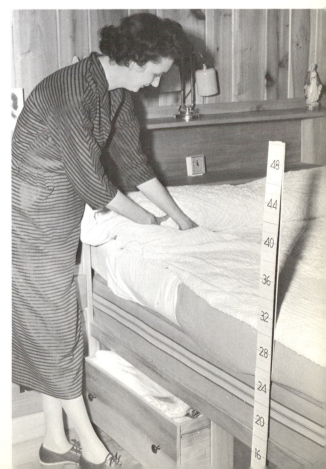

Research Methods in Planning Wheelchair Kitchens, Department of Home Economics, University of Illinois (I-81, 124)

There has been a great deal of research in various aspects of housing for the handicapped in many institutions here and abroad. A few projects are pictured in this chapter; many more are included in the bibliography.

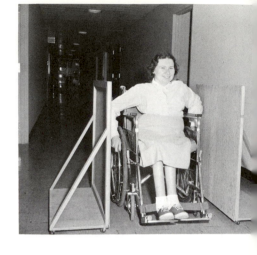

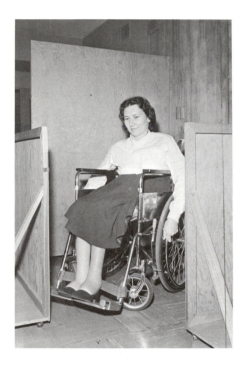

The method used to determine the space necessary to move forward and to turn a wheelchair is demonstrated by one of the twenty-six young women students in wheelchairs who participated in the research on wheelchair kitchens at the University of Illinois (I-81-82).

Kitchen equipment was tested for convenience in reach. Freezing compartments with the door hinged on the side proved practical, since it was possible to reach the contents from a sitting position. The drop-front type of door made the contents inaccessible from a seated position.

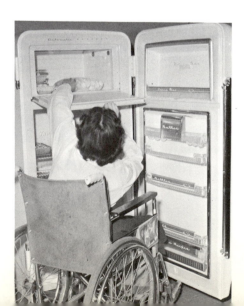

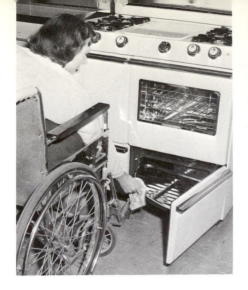

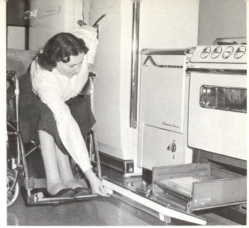

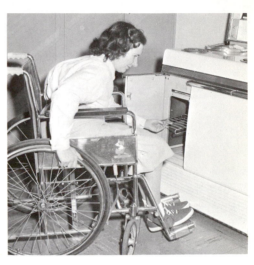

Convenience and safety in using various types of kitchen equipment were part of the University of Illinois research project. The study of broilers is pictured along with research on range of motion and convenience in storage.

The drop-down type proved to be too low and hazardous. The swing-out type was easier to use but also too low and hazardous. The side opening door for a broiler proved to be the easiest and safest to use.

Storage of the conventional type over a counter proved difficult to reach. A full-length cupboard with shallow shelves permits convenient storage space on six of the eight shelves.

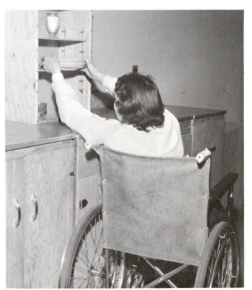

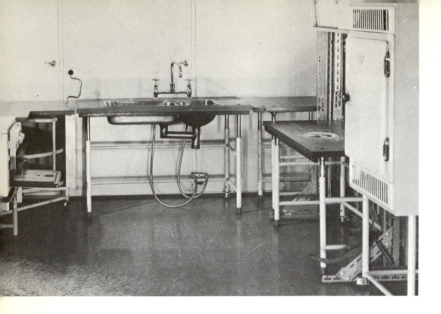

The Testing and Observation Institute of the Danish National Association for Infantile Paralysis

In Denmark, significant research on energy requirements for various tasks is being conducted under the direction of the Testing and Observation Institute of the Danish National Association for Infantile Paralysis. The first bulletin (1958) described tests "for estimating the relative working capacity of housewives doing housework." Since that time bulletins on energy studies have included other occupations. Bulletins number 3 and 6 deal with plans for homes for handicapped persons confined to wheelchairs (I-30, 80).

The test kitchen is completely mobile. All equipment is mounted on telescoping legs in order to facilitate raising and lowering to determine comfortable working heights.

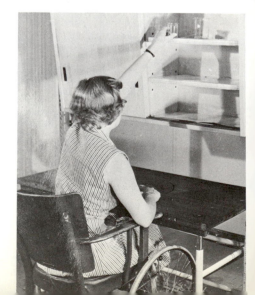

162

Research and Training in Homemaking
Sponsored by the Household Group of the
Swedish Central Committee for the Welfare of Cripples (S.V.C.K.)

Homemakers with disabilities of various kinds are brought to the "training flats" in various cities in Sweden to test kitchen layout, equipment, and devices, and to find methods suited to their particular needs. Before items are considered for testing, they must be approved from the point of view of workmanship and safety by the National Swedish Institute for Consumer Information (H).

Research programs in many areas of rehabilitation are directed by S.V.C.K. (I-52, 71, 123). The Household Group, one of the voluntary sub-committees since 1954, has stimulated far-reaching research and training projects in various aspects of homemaking in cooperation with the Swedish Foundation of Women's Organizations. They have also cooperated with the National Swedish Institute for Consumer Information in the development of clothing for handicapped women and for older people, and in other homemaking projects.

The Research Center on kitchen and bathroom planning and equipment in the S.V.C.K. headquarters near Stockholm has attracted visitors from all over the world. Results of research are reflected in the establishment of thirty "training flats" in various parts of Sweden which are patterned after the Stockholm flat established in 1957.

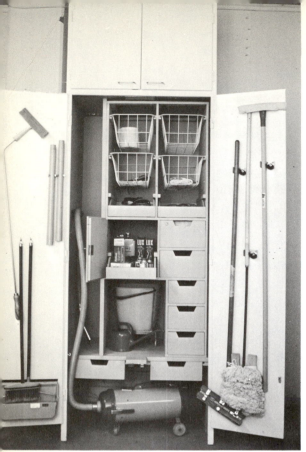

The design for the cleaning cabinet was developed from research on convenience and safety in household storage. It includes a locked cupboard for cleaning supplies and medicines that might be harmful to children.

Cluttered stairways are a common cause of home accidents (1-68). A well-organized storage cabinet would eliminate this hazard.

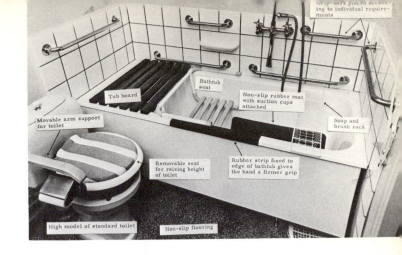

Grip-bars placed according to individual requirements

Bathtub seat

Tub board

Non-slip rubber mat with suction cups attached

Movable arm support for toilet

Soap and brush rack

Removable seat for raising height of toilet

Rubber strip fixed to edge of bathtub gives the hand a firmer grip

High model of standard toilet

Non-slip flooring

Research in Bathrooms for the Handicapped

The bathrooms installed in the Research Center of S.V.C.K. have many suggestions for convenience and safety to suit individual needs.

The shower nozzle (G-16) may be held in the hand while the person sits on the bathseat (G-8-9, 14, 17). It may also be hooked into a standard height bracket.

For new construction, wall-hung toilets (G-20) and basins should be considered, since they may be set at whatever height desired. This method of installation simplifies cleaning.

Swedish Folding Tub

A portable, folding, plastic bathtub in a metal frame may permit independence in bathing or it may provide a comfortable working height for the home nurse. The side can be lowered to permit easy transfer from crutches or from a wheelchair (G-29A).

The bottom of the tub is made of waterproof plywood and is covered with a waterproof mattress of foam rubber. The four standards that hold the sides of the tub fit into the base.

Regular shower plumbing fixtures are used to fill the tub. The shower nozzle, with a hand control, is on a flexible metal hose. The drain in the bottom empties into the permanent tub below.

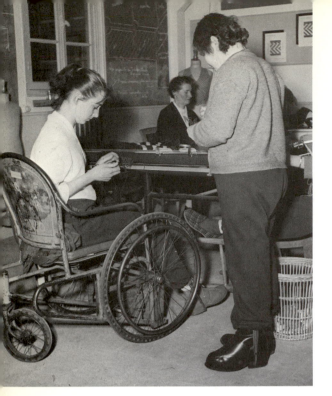

Research and Training in Homemaking at the Raymond Poincaré Hospital, Garches, France

Regardless of the type of disability, handicapped girls in the hospital of Garches, under the direction of the occupational therapist (who is also a physical therapist), have the satisfaction of participating in what the patients call "useful work." The hope of becoming even partially independent in homemaking tasks has great motivating power which is reflected in their perseverance in doing their required physical therapy exercises.

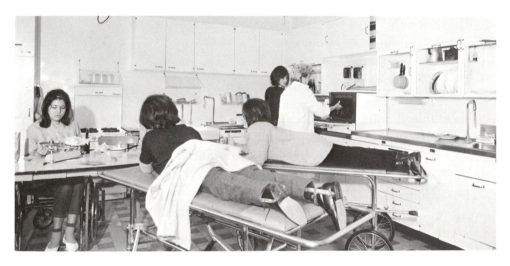

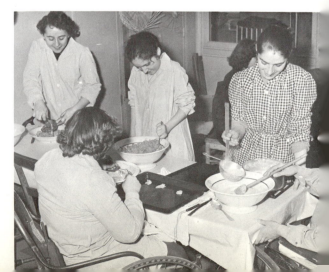

Research and Training in Homemaking at The Hague Rehabilitation Center

In the Netherlands, research and training in many types of rehabilitation is sponsored by the Nederlandse Centrale Vereniging voor Gebrekkigenzorg (I-34). This Rehabilitation Demonstration Center at The Hague is equipped with devices that enable homemakers with physical limitations to become more independent. Note especially:

The grab bar support beside the demonstration toilet (G-29).

The sink that allows knee room for wheelchairs.

The pull-out counter for stabilizing cooking utensils.

The carrier for the shopping bag.

The cabinet with toe room and swing-out shelves.

Research in housing is utilized in the energy-saving features in the "health houses" constructed for handicapped persons. Pictured are the "pass-through" from kitchen to dining room and the low-hung basin and mirror in the bedroom.

Research and Training in Homemaking in Great Britain

An extensive program of rehabilitation and housing for the handicapped is sponsored by hospitals and rehabilitation centers in many parts of the

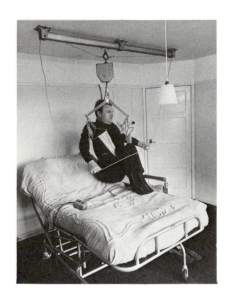

British Isles. Details on location and methods of financing are available through the Central Council for the Care of Cripples (H). The pioneering aspects of the program are represented by a bulletin on Homemaking for the Handicapped published as early as 1952 by the Department of Physical Medicine, Kings College Hospital in London (H). The Royal Devonshire Hospital at Buxton has a long established program for helping arthritic homemakers regain a maximum of independence (H).

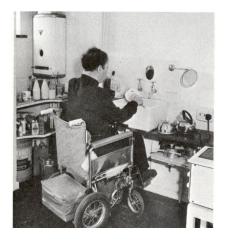

Examples of Housing for the Handicapped

In spite of severe physical limitations, this man lives as an independent member of his community. The electric hoist makes it possible for him to raise himself from a prone position and transfer himself to an electric wheelchair. The kitchen sink was raised to permit ample knee room; all of the cooking facilities are within easy reach. The sink is also used for shaving.

A low door sill and a platform outside of the front door makes it possible for him to leave his home in his electric chair, without assistance. Long handled tools permit him to manage his own small garden. The ramp leads to the sidewalk. Since the curb on the street has been eliminated, he is able to do his own shopping.

A Flat from a Housing Unit in Bromley, England

In determining the layout for the flat, the important areas were "mocked up" in hardboard in the contractor's workshop in order to get the minimum size to permit wheelchair traffic within the circulation area. Apart from the entrance foyer, there are no passages and perfect wheelchair circulation is available. This enables the person confined to a chair to be completely independent.

The working surfaces in the kitchen are set at a comfortable height and provide knee room. All supplies and equipment are within easy reach.

The bathroom is designed to give persons confined to wheelchairs a maximum of independence.

The window is operated by remote control teleflex gear; the control handle can be seen on the left wall.

The basin set at a comfortable height, has good shelf space, and it is shallow enough to allow room for the wheelchair.

The hot water heater is on the left wall and above it the infra-red room heater is fixed and operated by a pull cord switch.

The bath has a triangular shelf at the rear end to allow a wheelchair user to enter the bath by placing his legs on the shelf before easing himself into the bath. The pole grip and its horizontal bar allow for a variety of disabilities; a trapeze can be fixed to the horizontal bar if needed.

Bath water is controlled by a mixing valve seen on the side of the bath panel.

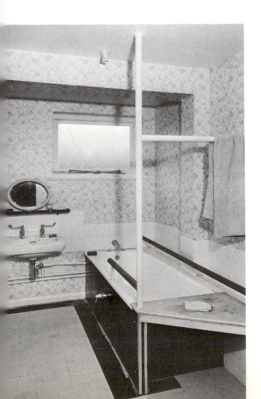
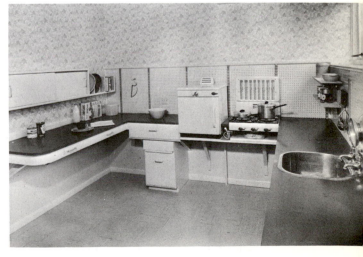

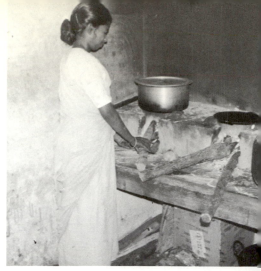

Research in Cooking Arrangements in India and Bangladesh

In many parts of the world cooking is done on the ground, both indoors and outdoors, with stones on the ground or on a cement base to support the cooking utensils. For indoor use, the fire box is often built into a cement bench at a good working height and a hood is built above which channels most of the smoke. One of the most satisfactory arrangements is the "smoke-less chula," which can be placed on a bench with storage cabinets underneath. A stove pipe carries off the smoke. The heat from the fire box circulates not only around the oven, but also under the three "burners," giving off a different intensity to each one.

Research and Training in Homemaking for the Handicapped in the United States

Several hundred pages would be necessary in order to report adequately on the programs in research and training for homemaker rehabilitation in the United States. Some examples appear in various chapters in this book and are listed in the photographic credits. The bibliography (I) gives a more comprehensive list. A few that have made special contributions to research are included in this chapter.

American Heart Association

The various branches of the American Heart Association have pioneered in both research and training for homemakers with low energy (I-50, 59, 64, 122). An example of the application of the research program appears in the kitchen-dining area pictured. Desirable features include: all working surfaces on the same level, single-control automatic mixer faucet for hot and cold water; hot water spray-rinse for dishes, to permit air drying rather than towel drying; storage areas on both sides of the counter; pantry with bamboo curtain on traverse rod that requires only a pull to put all supplies in plain sight and within easy reach.

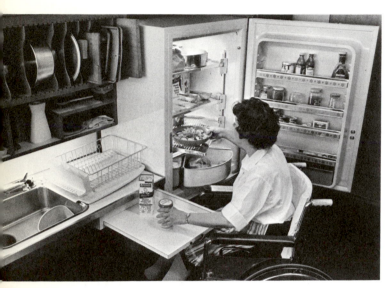

Institute of Physical Medicine and Rehabilitation
New York University Medical Center

The homemaker training unit at the Institute was one of the first efforts to combine research and training in homemaking. It serves as a demonstration for visitors from all over the world (I-63).

In addition to the wheelchair unit pictured, the kitchen has a standard height unit for ambulatory patients. Institute patients have an opportunity to work with staff to determine what changes will be necessary for them to work in their own home kitchens. A new Monograph (XXVII) describes the Kitchen Planning Service of the Institute and has pictures of adapted home kitchens (I-83-134).

Homemaking Areas in Rehabilitation Centers

The homemaker training kitchen in the Occupational Therapy Department in the Goodwill Industries Rehabilitation Center in Cincinnati is a good example of the homemaking areas in many rehabilitation centers in the United States. Good features include:

Cabinet shelves with a slanting front which permits storage closer to the counter.

Pull-out shelves in the base cabinet, pull-out pan racks, and corner Lazy Susan for convenient storage.

A continuous counter which permits the sliding of utensils and minimizes the amount of lifting necessary.

A sink with ample knee room set at a comfortable working height.

A work chair with large casters which fits under the sink.

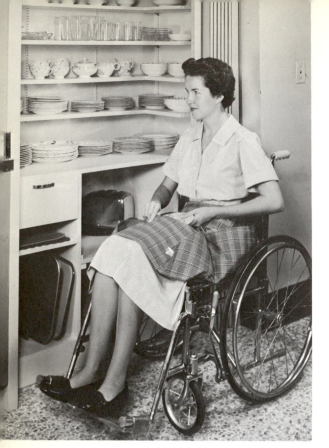

Clothing and Housing Research Division,
United States Department of Agriculture

For many years research that relates to
the home has been an important focus in
the United States Department of Agriculture and in the Land Grant Colleges
and State Universities. Hundreds of research reports are available, and although
much of the material is primarily concerned with the non-handicapped, it is
of value to all homemakers.[1]

As the result of the U.S. Department
of Agriculture research in energy con-
sumption, a number of bulletins on
kitchen planning have been published
(I-72-79, 129). Pictured here is the storage cabinet in the dining area of the
kitchen and also the planning area and
play center in the kitchen-workroom.

[1] For lists of publications in the area of special
interest, write the Government Printing Office
(H) and the Home Economics Extension Service of your State University.

CHAPTER 12

Independent Living
at Any Age

Choosing a Place to Live

Previous chapters in this book have demonstrated how a person with physical limitations may apply the principles of work simplification to his clothing problems and housekeeping chores and thus achieve his maximum degree of independence. Just where he will live will depend on circumstances, but hopefully he will have some choice. One of the appealing possibilities, to many, is to continue to live in the familiar neighborhood and in the old family home. If a compromise is necessary it may be possible to set aside a part of the house as an apartment for rental purposes. A carefully chosen tenant might not only supplement the income but also provide extra security by having "someone in the house."

A "grandparents' apartment" attached to the home of a son or daughter, or some other family member, may be the answer for some. Facilities that are completely separate can help avoid friction and will offer a maximum of independence to all concerned. If the shift can be made while the grandparents are still vigorous, they would then have a better opportunity to "take root" and develop a new life of their own. Some people choose to live in apartments, hotels, or condominiums where the burden of maintenance is taken over by the management. They may also have the advantage of having a restaurant on the property.

People on limited income, whether they be elderly or physically disabled, or both, may find comfortable quarters in municipal housing projects. Those who are veterans may qualify for one of the "domiciliaries" operated by the Veteran's Administration. Churches and fraternal organizations have been sponsoring special housing projects for their members for many years. Some include cottages and apartments built around a central dining area and social

Following a romance which started in a Sheltered Workshop these young people were married and set up housekeeping in a trailer. The ramp was arranged to give easy access to the car. Crutches are seldom necessary inside the trailer. They are both able to use foot power to operate narrow chairs with ball bearing casters, thus enabling them to move about in the living- dining- kitchen area. An assortment of railings and grips, set up to suit their particular needs, make it possible for them to walk into the hall, bedroom, and bath.

center. Additional security is offered when provision has been made for nursing care and an infirmary.

There are all kinds of retirement communities and private retirement homes. Many have a wide range of services as well as recreational and cultural activities. The fact that everyone in the community is "65 or over" and that families with children are not admitted, is to some an advantage.

People who like easy-to-care-for housing may consider a mobile home. The investment is considerably smaller than in the case of most houses. Satisfaction depends, in part, on the arrangement of the interior and the amount of private outside space, but more important is the location and the availability of shopping and health services.

Cooperative housing is the choice of many people in all age groups and with various degrees of mobility. Many consider this plan a happy alternative to institutional care since it is possible to share expenses for housekeeping services and for attendants. As in all cooperative plans, the success depends on the people concerned as well as on careful preliminary planning, mutual understanding, and a high degree of tolerance.

Several countries are developing experimental villages in which persons with physical limitations "run the town." They literally hold all of the offices and provide all services possible. The best plan would be to have this type of development close to and integrated with a more cosmopolitan community.

Barrier-Free Living

For those who travel in wheelchairs, a well constructed ramp is a prerequisite for independence.

How long will we continue to shut some people out?

*The International Symbol of Access. The "wel-
come in" sign for the handicapped.*

"Barrier-free" communities are still in the dream stage in many areas, but
there has been significant progress in the past twenty years in making public
buildings accessible to all, with the construction of ramps, the widening of
doors, the installation of elevators and in making telephones, drinking foun-
tains and rest rooms available to persons with physical limitations.

Many buildings both here and abroad now display the International Symbol of Access which indicates that the area is accessible to persons on crutches
or those who travel in wheel chairs or are physically limited in other ways.[1]

[1] Contact your state Governor's Committee on Employment of the Handicapped for
copies of the International "Symbol of Access" and for a directory of barrier-free buildings and recreation areas.

An assortment of travel guide books, local, state and national, is now available. They designate barrier-free buildings and areas of interest as well as suitable rest stops along the highway.[1]

Along with the program to make public buildings and educational and cultural centers available to persons with physical limitations, there has been tremendous progress in developing barrier-free recreational opportunities in local communities and in state and national parks and forests. These are multipurpose facilities arranged to serve all of the people. Fishing piers are made wide enough to admit wheel chairs and swimming areas are made accessible to all. Parts of nature trails are hard surfaced so that they may be traveled by persons in wheelchairs as well as those who are blind and also by the non-handicapped.

Benches are provided for people with limited energy who like to just sit and rest and listen. Guidelines along almost any trail make it possible for blind persons to travel them independently. Various experiments are in progress to find suitable ways to provide interpretive notes. Some signs are done in braille as well as in conventional letters.

Multipurpose trails can be used by everyone, including the blind and those who must travel in wheelchairs or use crutches.

"Ski touring" offers an opportunity to explore the *"winter wonderland."* This is one of the winter sports open to many people regardless of age, and is considered much safer than skiing.

Winter sports furnish a special kind of pleasure and sense of achievement for ski touring enthusiasts of any age and to skiers and snowmobilers regardless of their physical limitations. The excitement of a "one-track" ski race is described well in this excerpt from an article by Steve Schuster:

> From where we stood at the bottom of the slope, the line of skiers racing down toward us looked pretty much like any group of good skiers. Nice form . . . real smooth. Then we sort of "froze" when they came into full view. All these guys—even their instructor—was missing either an arm or leg! I guess we knew what to expect . . . but actually seeing amputees ski . . . is something else![2]

---

[2] "If I Can Do This—I Can Do Anything," *Snow Sports*, December 1969, pp. 17–18.

"If I can do this, I can do anything!" That's
the reaction of amputees who try out for snowmobiling and "one track" skiing.

Here is a demonstration of courage, determination, skill, ingenuity, and independence. This young veteran was one of the many young men wounded in Vietnam. His injury was such that both of his legs had to be amputated above the knee. This picture was taken at the National Morgan Cutting Horse Finals where he won first prize in open competition. His short stirrups are leather cones designed to fit his stumps and are lined with sheepskin. He wears a car safety belt fastened to the saddle.

Private Transportation

Fortunate is the person who has his own car adapted to his particular disability and who lives in an area that has special parking for the handicapped. This is also true if the person has a van that will admit a wheelchair and has a push-button controlled ramp or a hydraulic lift. An assortment of slings or grips may be necessary to insure his safety and independence. If the mechanics of operating the van have also been adjusted to suit his needs, he is really "in the driver's seat" for local and cross country trips. With the proper overnight equipment, he can be completely independent.

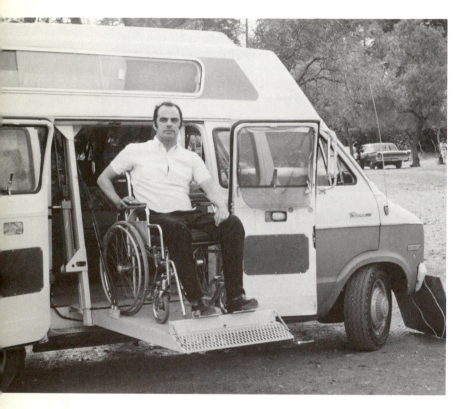

This young man is representative of a growing number of quadriplegics who have worked out new ways of becoming independent and have become active, contributing citizens. The van, equipped with special controls and a push-button hydraulic lift, makes it possible for him to get around the town and also to take his family on long trips.

The development of recreational vehicles has opened a whole world of possibilities for the elderly and handicapped. One can travel with complete independence and comfort, even luxury, without searching for "special" accommodations along the way. They may also serve as ideal vacation cottages or as a convenient guest room when visiting families and friends. They, like permanent homes, should be selected with care. Especially helpful are those with open floor space for ease in getting around, wide doorways, and sliding, folding, or rollaway cupboard doors which do not get in the way.

Public Transportation

This train with a wide entrance on platform level is a far cry from the old fashioned type with narrow steep steps.

Planes, trains, busses and taxis are all becoming more accessible to handicapped travelers. Some trains now have wide doors *on platform level* and wide aisles to permit easy access for wheelchairs. Airlines vary in ways to accommodate the traveler with physical limitations but it is well to make arrangements in advance. There are some that organize tours of handicapped persons. "Handicabs" are part of the "taxi-bus" service in some communities. They operate on a schedule and their great advantage is that they are especially adapted for the use of those who travel in wheelchairs.

The "Handicab", operating on a regular schedule, is an important part of independent living. Similar services are offered in some communities by a new vehicle called a "Transbus."

Community Services

In every state there are tax-supported and voluntary agencies at work on various projects designed to help the handicapped and elderly to become as independent as possible. Organizations differ in each state but all are worth exploring. Home care rather than institutional care for the chronically ill is the objective in many of the programs. Organizations such as the Visiting Nurse Association and the Homemaker-Health Aide Service are among the agencies that make up the health and welfare team.

A program from a London hospital for the chronically ill is worthy of exploration. The plan has the patient spend three weeks in the hospital where he is given intensive training in independent living. He then spends three weeks at home and is encouraged to practice being as independent as possible. He then returns to the hospital for another three-week stay. This plan permits the hospital to care for twice as many patients and relieves the family of responsibility for a part of the time. It also gives the patient a welcome change of scene.

186

Meals on Wheels

This nutrition program originated in Great Britain and is designed to provide people in need with a daily hot meal, an important supplement to the diet of those who have lost the incentive to prepare more than the "tea and toast" type of meal. The program is in operation in many communities in the U.S.

Good Neighbor Programs

Urban communities are beginning to follow the good neighbor practices that have been a part of our rural mountain culture since pioneer days. The urban "friendly visitors" program is similar to the rural custom of having a neighbor "come and set for a while" and perhaps bring "a little something." The rural telephone call to those who are "feeling poorly" has its urban counterpart in the "ring-a-day" plan. Urban young people, organized to do odd jobs for those in need, are a variation of the groups of young people in rural areas who naturally expect to "help out" anyone who "can't get around."

Volunteer Work and Paid Employment

The biblical advice on it being "more blessed to give than to receive" applies especially to the person with physical limitations. Having something to give or share is for many a necessary part of life. Even the "shut-ins" need not be *shutout*." They can be enlisted to assist in all kinds of community programs and some paid jobs where the chief needs are determination, some extra energy, and a convincing voice. Telephones can be rigged to suit almost any type of disability.

The "shut-in" need not be "shut-out" when there is ingenuity in adjusting a telephone.

What does a teacher do when she retires? She joins R.S.V.P. and does the thing she loves best to do.

Literally hundreds of national voluntary agencies and church organizations are looking for volunteers for various kinds of projects that involve the telephone. The local United Fund office can suggest agencies in need of help. A new tax-supported organization, The National Center For Voluntary Action can offer suggestions gathered from all over the United States.

Retirement from industry to R.S.V.P. and a "second career" as driver of a day care center bus, has unanticipated satisfactions.

ACTION is another tax-supported agency which provides an assortment of interesting opportunities, some volunteer and some paid, for community services both in the United States and in foreign countries. The familiar ones are the Peace Corps for foreign service, where age is an asset, and Vista, which includes programs to help the underprivileged in the United States. Some of the other opportunities include R.S.V.P., the Retired Senior Volunteer Program, and S.C.O.R.E., the Service Corps of Retired Executives. The national ACTION program also includes the appealing Foster Grandparents Program which, as the name implies, has mutual benefits.

As far as regular paid jobs are concerned, there are local, state, and national organizations designed to increase opportunities for those with physical limitations. In every county in the United States, there are branch offices of the Rehabilitation Services Administration where free vocational appraisal, training, and placement assistance are available. Federal employment offices are also scattered all over the country and in some communities there are special representatives from the Veterans Administration to assist veterans in finding employment. The twenty-five-year-old, non-partisan President's Committee on Employment of the Handicapped has its counterpart in every state, in the Governor's Committee on Employment of the Handicapped, located at the state capital. This committee has a knowledge of opportunities for the employment of the handicapped and offers suggestions free of charge.

Money Savers

Frugal people will find money-saving opportunities worth exploring. Many drugstores offer discounts for prescription drugs to people "65 or over." This is also true of some car rental services. Aside from income tax reductions, because of age or certain types of disability, there are also property tax reductions for people in some income brackets. Hotels often offer special rates for retired educators and some have discounts for anyone who is 65 or over. In some parts of Europe and the United States, there are transportation discounts in planes, trains, and busses for people 65 and over, including foreigners. In some educational institutions, tuition is free to veterans and to people in the older age group. Some theaters and other places of entertainment offer ticket discounts. *The New York Times* offers a discount to A.A.R.P. members in a *Large Type Weekly Edition.*

How to Keep Alive as Long as You Live

There is now an increasing emphasis on physical exercise as a prerequisite for health at any age or with almost any type of physical limitation. National, state, and local organizations are available to promote practically any kind of sport.

In or out of a wheelchair, competition is fun. The National Wheelchair Athletic Association promotes a wide variety of sports.

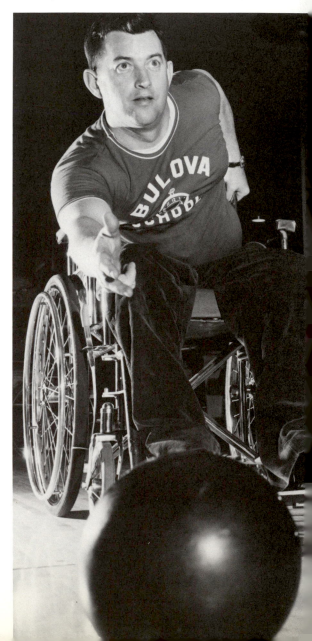

This 90-year-old bowler played her first game two years ago. She says it is a good way to have fun and to keep physically fit.

These two have been companions on many trails. The rider is 84 and his Arabian stallion, 24 years old.

Gardening is a joy for many people of all ages. The garden may be a conventional one, a raised flower bed, or a window sill. Bending is no longer necessary. New tools with longer handles save the back and the knees. Flower boxes can be set up in tiers for "vertical gardening" when garden space is not available or when the gardener has difficulty in bending. New instruction books and tools for gardeners with physical limitations are now on the market.

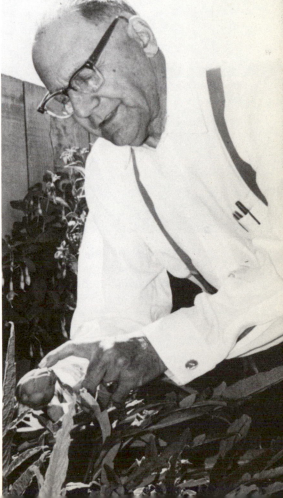

Just as physical fitness can be maintained only through proper nutrition and exercise, mental and spiritual growth are also dependent on stimulation and activity. Many educational institutions welcome people of any age who want to learn. Many city libraries have bookmobiles that travel to surrounding areas and some have home service. The Library of Congress can supply information on "Talking Books," (phonograph records) for the blind and the handicapped.

Time to "do the thing you always wanted to do" is one of the dividends of having survived long enough to be in that "older age group." Hobbies offer a fine opportunity for study and a chance to associate with people of all ages who have similar interests.

The development of hobbies and "doing the thing one always wanted to do" often takes study. One big advantage is that hobbies offer an opportunity to associate with people *from all age groups on the basis of a common interest.* The old saying about not being able to "teach an old dog new tricks" may apply to dogs but research has proved that with interest and effort *a person can learn at any age.*

Good aging is not merely a quest for comfort and contentment but the acceptance by the aging person of a difficult challenge to meet new problems, face new difficulties, attain new levels of maturity and especially to be more truly himself than ever before. To do this fully he must have a clear sense of purpose, for only purpose can give significance to his efforts . . . Without purpose his efforts to adjust are likely to be shadowed by a sense of aimlessness which robs them of their vitality.[3]

There is a quantity of biographical evidence to prove that people with physical limitations can achieve in astonishing ways in their hobbies or in second careers. The secret may lie in the words of this quotation:

> God grant me the serenity
> to accept the things I cannot change;
> Courage to change the things I can;
> And wisdom to know the difference.

[3] Elliott Dunlap Smith, *Handbook of Aging, For Those Growing Old and Those Concerned with Them*, (New York: Harper & Row, 1972), p. 104.

CHAPTER 13

Learning to Live
with Physical Limitations

There is unfortunately no neat set of scientifically proven principles to simplify the task of learning how to live with a disability. Success depends largely on the inner resources of the individual, his attitude toward his limitations, and the support and encouragement he may receive from his family and friends.

For all of us, with or without visible disabilities, the constant, continuous problem of learning to manage ourselves is far more difficult than learning to manage a home. Moreover, the two problems are very closely related—the degree of achievement in one area is reflected in the other.

A person with a handicap has all of the problems of a non-handicapped person plus one—his own particular physical limitations. *No one is better able than he to advise others on how to learn to live with physical limitations provided that he has succeeded in winning his own battle.* All of us might profit from the following advice.

Try to Accept the Limitations You Can't Change

Just as you accept the fact that you have brown eyes or that you need to wear glasses, learn to accept your physical limitations. After a certain point there isn't much you can do about eliminating your physical handicap. Take stock of your assets and go on from there.

Try to Avoid Feeling Sorry for Yourself

If you go about with a "poor me—poor me" attitude, it will be not only devastating for you but will also tax the patience of your family and friends. The people around you will generally react as you give them the cue. If you discourage the "you poor thing" attitude, they will gradually think of you as a "person" and not as a "handicapped person."

Don't Limit Yourself Unduly, but Be Realistic!

Remember we all have untapped potential. Try to do everything you possibly can within the limitations of your handicap, but don't waste your energy in doing something that really isn't important just to prove you can do it! There is no single "right" way to do a job. The problem is to discover the best way for you to do it. This means experimentation and persistence and a substantial amount of courage!

Don't Hesitate to Admit Failure; No One Has a 100 Per Cent Score!

Trial and error are a part of any learning process. Learn to laugh at your own failures and encourage others to laugh with you; it will help to ease disappointments and will give you the courage to try again. If you finally find that a job is too difficult or impossible, or takes too large a proportion of your time and energy, just admit it, ask for help, and try something else.

Begin with Goals That Are Not Too High

Be realistic! Progress comes by inches! Have the satisfaction of mastering a small, not-too-difficult job, and then pick a bigger one. Physical and psychological adjustment does not come in a week or even a year.

Learn to Deal Kindly with the Curiosity of Others

People are often amazingly curious about a disability and often ask very embarrassing questions, sometimes in public where you know all eyes are on you! This will happen again and again, so you had better think up a stock answer that doesn't invite more questions and also try to develop a "thick skin." People really do not mean to be unkind but are merely thoughtless, and many are totally lacking in the capacity to put themselves into the place of a handicapped person.

Learn to Accept Kindness and Attention Graciously!

Aside from your family and friends there are few people who will be aware of your struggle for independence, nor can they know when you are able to manage things alone. The first impulse of many people when they see an obvious handicap is to try to help. They seldom realize their efforts may be entirely unnecessary or even dangerous to the handicapped person. Try hard to be gracious! Accept an offer of help in the spirit in which it is given; this is one way you can give others the feeling they have done something useful!

Make Use of Community Services

Never before have there been so many tax-supported and private agencies concerned with the elderly and the handicapped. Get acquainted with them (H) and perhaps they can give you just the extra help or advice you need.

Think of Something You Can Do for Someone Else

No one can be happy unless he is giving as well as receiving. This may start in some simple way—perhaps by making some little thing or doing something for a member of the family. There are also many volunteer jobs in every community that can be done by a person who for some reason is "home-bound." It may be a job that involves telephoning or mailing or it may be serving as a leader of a youth organization that meets right in your own home. *Don't be "shut out" just because you are "shut in"!*

Your future will be determined not so much by the nature of your disability as by what you do with what you have left.

Some Advice from a Person with Physical Limitations to Family and Friends

Don't rush me with a lot of your ideas for my rehabilitation until I have time to "pull myself together." It will take a little while for me to face reality. Let's plan together.

Try to think of me as a "person with a handicap" and not as a handicapped person. This will help me to get over the feeling of being "different." I will need some looking after and I do appreciate all that you do for me, but don't smother my small efforts toward independence or kill my initiative by being overly protective.

Encourage me to try to do everything that *I want to try.*

Always remember that my disabilities are only physical—not mental. Help me to concentrate on what I *can* do rather than be too concerned over what I *cannot* do!

Give me responsibility as soon as I am able to assume it. I may be ready sooner than you think.

Of course my disability has been a terrific shock for me, but I know it has been a shock for you, too. It will take a lot of adjustments all around and plenty of tolerance and patience, understanding and cooperation.

There is an Indian prayer which says, "Great Spirit, grant that I may not judge my neighbor until I have walked a mile in his moccasins." Perhaps we should *exchange moccasins once in a while.*

Adaptation of Equipment
for Child Care

Construction of Bathing and Dressing Center for Use of Mother Confined to a Wheelchair

Dressing Table

Procedure (measurements to be determined by size of wheelchair and space available; approximately 64″ x 31″ x 18″):

Add drawer stops and large oversize knobs to drawers of small chest.

Construct L-shaped leg to conform in size to chest. Adjust height to insure under-the-top clearance for arms of wheelchair.

Fashion top of ¾″ plywood, allowing width to permit knee room for working in a forward position, and screw to leg and chest.

Cover foam rubber pad with terry cloth.

Add safety strap with grippers or Velcro.

Fasten pad to table with elastic.

Mobile Wheel Cart Base for Tub

Construct frame of tubular aluminum about 26″ high to fit plastic tub equipped with drain. (High enough to allow knee room for mother.)

Add 3″ swivel casters.

When frame is no longer used for baby bathing, it may be converted into an excellent wheeled cart.

Construct tray of ¾″ plywood to fit securely over the top of the frame.

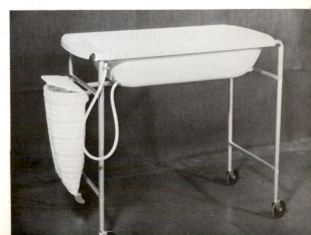

Adaptation of Chest of Drawers to Serve as Storage Area for a Mother Who Stands to Bathe and Dress Her Baby

This stacked dressing unit is made by building a chest for the baby clothes to be placed on top of a conventional general-purpose chest of drawers.

After the child is ready to help to dress himself, the upper chest can be equipped with legs and doors and placed on floor level.

Procedure for Lower Chest Adaptation

Begin with a secondhand sturdy chest of drawers.

Add nylon glides to drawers for easy operation.

Add towel racks for drawer pulls for long drawers to facilitate opening with one hand.

Substitute easy-to-grasp screen door handles for knobs on small drawers.

Procedure for Constructing Upper Chest

Construct the top chest of plywood to the size of the old chest, 30-36" high.

Fit one side with adjustable shelves, the other with a rod for hanging clothing.

Add curtains on drapery cranes.

Procedure for Adapting Upper Chest for Child's Wardrobe

Lift off upper chest.

Add four legs to raise it about 12" off the floor so that it is easily accessible for the child.

Curtains may be replaced by doors with magnetic catches.

202

Adaptation of Cribs to Suit
the Needs of Mothers with Physical Limitations

Adjusting Toe-Trip Bar to Lower Side of Crib

Mothers in wheelchairs frequently find it difficult to lower the side of the crib with the toe-trip bar. When this mechanism is reversed, it can be pushed inward and operated by the hand.

PROCEDURE

Remove the front side of crib by removing the two rod guides and latching plate.

Saw off angular lock part of the latching plate and smooth down.

Replace the plate.

Reverse side of crib when replacing it so trip bar will operate by being pushed inward.

Adjusting Height of Mattress

To minimize lifting, the mattress may be raised by placing a wooden frame under it. This same idea can be used in carriages and bassinets.

PROCEDURE

Cut two stringers slightly less than crib length and three-fourths the desired elevating distance.

Cut three cross ties slightly less than crib width and the same width as stringers.

Cut ¼″ notches in the stringers and panels to the midline of each panel.

Sand each piece, cover with shellac, and paint.

Cut plywood platform slightly smaller than bottom of the crib.

Sand, shellac, and paint.

Interlock cross ties and stringers.

Place platform on top of stringers and mattress on the platform.

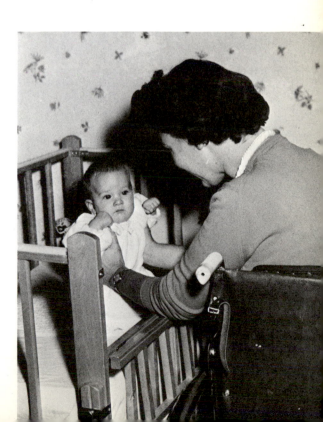

Construction of a Mobile Dressing Cart

Materials Needed

Student desk (secondhand), Plywood for shelf (¾″), Suitable drawers from discarded chest, Plywood for blocking in drawers (¼″), Set of 5″ rubber casters (2 rigid, 2 swivel with brakes), 2 sturdy round towel rods (approx. ⅝″ diameter), 3′ length of 3/16″ rod, Drawer glides for four drawers, 4 large drawer pulls, Foam rubber pad with cover, 4 yds. plastic-coated material to make pockets on back of cart, laundry bag, and safety strap of plastic-coated material lined with 3″ elastic webbing, 6″ Velcro or 2 grippers.

PROCEDURE

Make the large single drawer into two drawers. (To permit access to the drawer as well as to provide support of the drawer handle for balance.)

Insert the plywood shelf on leg braces.

Install additional drawers and fit with drawer glides for smooth operation.

Substitute screen door handles for knobs.

Use 5″ casters to raise the cart to height of sink to be used for bathing.

Install sturdy towel rods on each end to serve as support as well as handles.

Bend the rod into a square, with a pin to fit the hinge leaf, to make the laundry bag holder.

Make laundry bag to fit square frame.

Raise the back strip by attaching an additional board and fitting with a pocketed slip cover of the plastic-coated fabric.

Cover the surface foam rubber pad with a plastic cover.

Attach a safety strap of plastic-coated material lined with elastic webbing. Fasten with Velcro fastening or grippers.

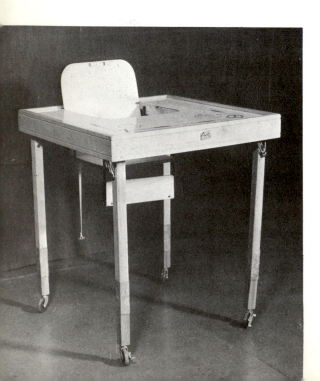

Adaptation to Raise Height of Feeding Table

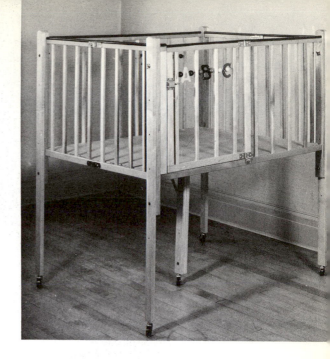

Materials Needed

Commercial feeding table (wood), Hardwood stock to match dimensions of legs, 20-gauge galvanized sheet metal, 2 swivel and 2 lock 2″ casters.

PROCEDURE

Remove old casters.

Cut leg extensions to desired height including casters.

Insert casters in extensions.

Fashion metal sleeves to fit legs and solder.

Add sleeves and extensions to feeding table to bring to desired height.

Adaptations of Play Pen
Converting a Low Play Pen into a High Play Pen

PROCEDURE

Cut 24″ gate into rigid side of pen.

Add bottom rail to form gate.

Fasten hinges in center.

Fasten latch on post side.

Cut legs the maximum height desired.

Drill holes 6″ apart in old and new legs.

Position nuts and bolts to desired height.

Replace center leg.

Add casters.

Materials Needed

Commonly used play pen — ¼″ carriage bolts with wing nuts — Hardwood stock to match play pen legs — Pair 1″ narrow butt hinges — Collar sash lock — 5 composition full-swivel 2″ stem casters.

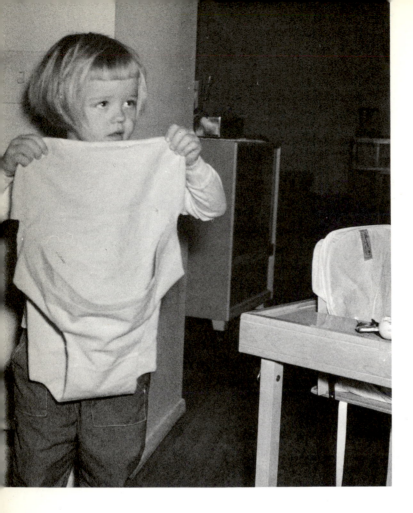

"Safety Slip Cover" for a Child's Chair

Conventional safety straps on feeding tables, car seats, and highchairs are often impossible for mothers with hand limitations to fasten. A "safety slip cover" will keep the child from slipping out or from standing up in the chair.

PROCEDURE

Construct a simple slip cover to fit about 6 or 8 inches over the back of the child's car seat or chair and attach it to roomy pants (similar to the canvas seats in walkers, swings, etc.). This will require approximately 1 yard of sturdy, washable fabric. The mother can put her child into the pants of this safety slip cover while he is still in the crib, place him in the chair and put the back of the slip cover over the back of the chair or seat without too much difficulty.

Adaptation of Household Equipment

Adaptation of Standard 36″ Metal Kitchen-Cabinet-Type Sink to a Comfortable Working Height for the Person Confined to a Wheelchair

Materials

Any standard cabinet model steel sink — 2 x 3 fir stock — ⅛″ pegboard or ¼″ plywood.

PROCEDURE

Construct a cross-supported framework by using 2 x 3″ stock, with legs short enough to give approximately a 31″ sink rim height. Front leg area should be cut back to provide a space 9″ high and 6″ deep to accommodate wheelchair foot rests. The entire inside should be kept open for knee room. If the drainboard is long enough, there may be room for a wheel cart to be stored underneath. A piece of pegboard fastened to the end will provide room for a narrow shelf or hooks for hanging items used at the sink.

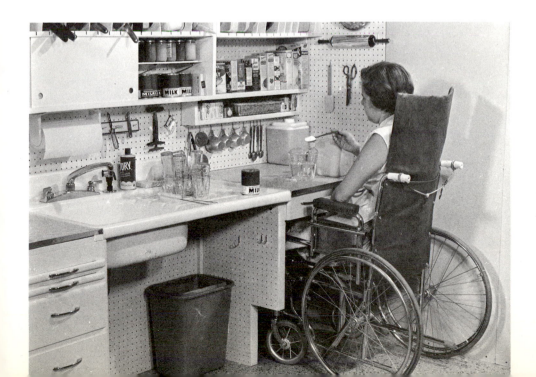

The top of a standard metal cabinet sink can be lifted off and placed on the frame.

It is desirable to install plumbing as far back as possible to allow knee room and also minimize danger of burning.

Adaptations for the "Sit-to-Work" Chair

Materials Needed

A comfortable, old chair, Set of four plate-type rubber wheel swivel casters, ¾" plywood, 1 x 1" material for rim.

PROCEDURE

Cut off legs of chair so that when placed on a castered platform the seat
    height will be about 18" high.
Construct a platform to conform to the chair leg spread.
Cut back heel space on platform.
Finish edges with a slight rim by using 1 x 1" strips.
Add casters.
Position chair on top and fasten.
Rubber tubing may be tacked around the platform to serve as a bumper.

Device for Lifting Wheelchair into Trunk of Automobile

Clothing Research and Development Foundation, Inc., Helen Cookman, Executive Director, 48 East 66th Street, New York, New York 10021.

Fashion-Able, Rocky Hill, New Jersey 08553.

Leinenweber, Inc., Custom Tailors, Brunswick Bldg., 69 W. Washington St., Chicago, Illinois 60602.

Vocational Guidance and Rehabilitation Service, 2239 East 55th Street, Cleveland, Ohio 44103.

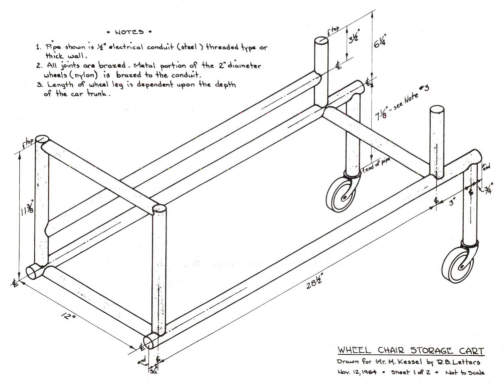

• NOTES •

1. Pipe shown is ½" electrical conduit (steel) threaded type or thick wall.
2. All joints are brazed. Metal portion of the 2" diameter wheels (nylon) is brazed to the conduit.
3. Length of wheel leg is dependent upon the depth of the car trunk.

WHEEL CHAIR STORAGE CART
Drawn for Mr. M. Kessel by R.B. Letters
Nov. 12, 1964 • Sheet 1 of 2 • Not to Scale

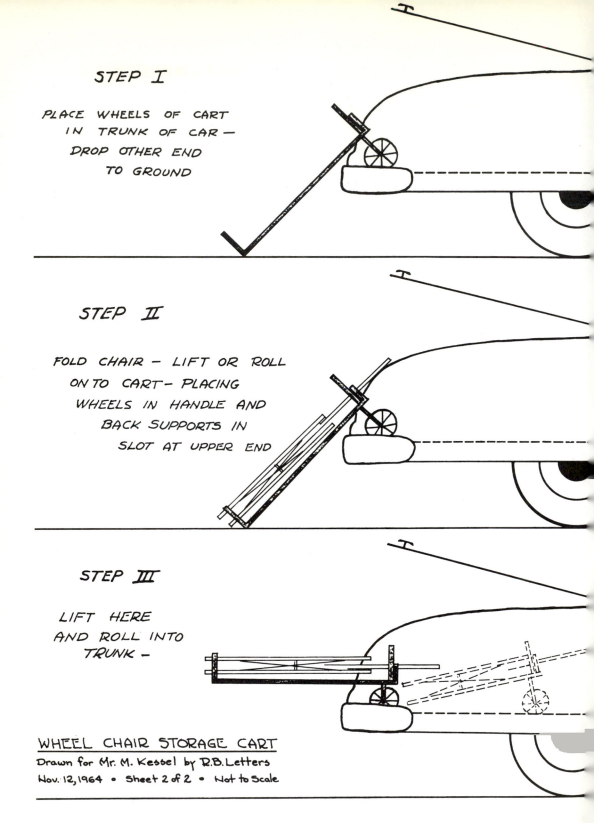

STEP I

PLACE WHEELS OF CART
IN TRUNK OF CAR —
DROP OTHER END
TO GROUND

STEP II

FOLD CHAIR — LIFT OR ROLL
ON TO CART — PLACING
WHEELS IN HANDLE AND
BACK SUPPORTS IN
SLOT AT UPPER END

STEP III

LIFT HERE
AND ROLL INTO
TRUNK —

WHEEL CHAIR STORAGE CART

Drawn for Mr. M. Kessel by R.B. Letters
Nov. 12, 1964 • Sheet 2 of 2 • Not to Scale

Directions for Making
Clothing Adaptations

Crotch Openings on Overalls or Trousers

1. Open the inseam the entire length and cuffs if there are cuffs on the pants.
2. Plain seams are easier to adapt than flat fell seams.
3. Insert zipper into seam. The zipper should be one inch shorter than the length of the opening.
4. Both ends of the zipper should be reinforced.
5. The cuff should be stitched back to hold it in place.

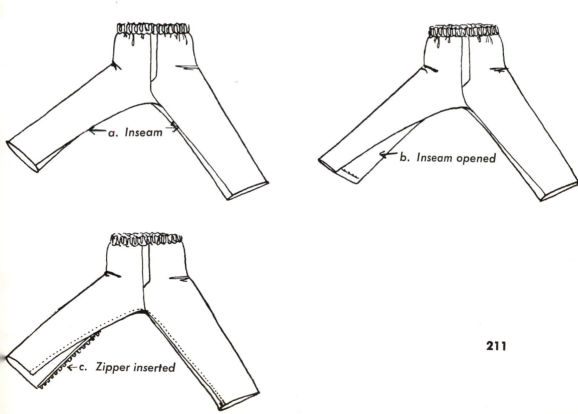

a. Inseam

b. Inseam opened

c. Zipper inserted

211

Raising the Armhole in a Sleeveless Garment

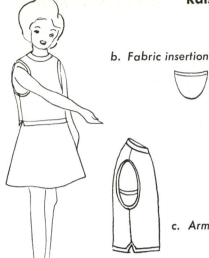

b. Fabric insertion

1. Cut a curved piece of fabric in matching or contrasting fabric. Four pieces will be needed.
2. Stitch two pieces together across the top on the wrong side and trim and turn to the right side.
3. Insert finished piece in the armhole and stitch in place.
4. Repeat the process for the other armhole.

c. Armhole raised by fabric insertion

a. Armhole cut too deep for body build

Velcro Opening on the Inseam of Trousers

1. Open the inseam from the cuff to desired length. The length will vary with the length of the braces.
2. Press seam allowance on back of leg flat.
3. Stitch loop side of Velcro on top of seam allowance.
4. Stitch hook side to front seam allowance. The front seam allowance is turned back and pressed before Velcro is inserted.
5. Reinforce ends of Velcro with double stitching.
6. Stitch cuffs in place.

Zipper plackets can also be converted to Velcro by removing the zipper and inserting strips of Velcro. The loop side of the Velcro is stitched to the under part of the placket and the hook side to the top lap of the placket.

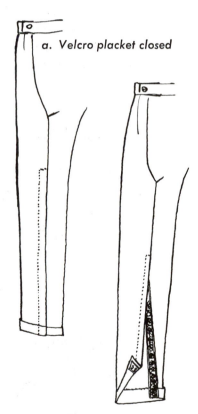

a. Velcro placket closed

b. Velcro placket opened

212

Front-Opening Bra

1. Back opening of bra is closed and stitched.
2. Center front seam of bra is cut open.
3. The hook side of bra "refresher" pack is inserted on one side of the opening and stitched twice for added strength.
4. The eye side of bra "refresher" pack is attached to the other side of the opening.

Bra "refresher" packs are available in different sizes; there are one-hook, two-hook, or three-hook fasteners.

a. Open seam at center front.

b. Bra "refresher" pack

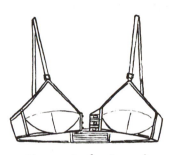

c. New center front opening

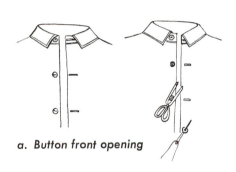

a. Button front opening

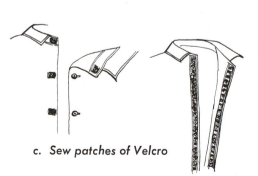

b. Cut off buttons. Stitch button over buttonhole

c. Sew patches of Velcro

d. Sew strips of Velcro

Converting a Button Opening to a Velcro Opening

1. Remove buttons and sew buttons over buttonholes to keep the garment appearance the same.
2. Cut squares or strips of Velcro.
3. Sew loop side of Velcro to the original button side of the garment.
4. Sew hook side of Velcro under the buttonholes on the inside of the garment.

Strips of Velcro may be used in place of squares; however, the shirt will be bulkier.

Cuffs on Shirts

Velcro Fastener

1. Remove buttons and place over buttonholes.
2. Sew squares of Velcro on cuffs, loop side on back cuff and hook side on front cuff.
3. Cuff closes with a pat or by rolling arm along a hard surface.

Elastic Cuff Links

1. Join two buttons together with elastic thread.
2. Make a machine buttonhole on back cuff.
3. Insert cuff link into buttonholes.

The cuff link will expand and provide enough room for the hand to slip through without fastening the cuff.

APPENDIX E

Clothing Sources

Clothing Research and Development Foundation, Inc., Helen Cookman, Executive Director, 48 East 66th Street, New York, New York 10021.

Fashion-Able, Rocky Hill, New Jersey 08553.

Leinenweber, Inc., Custom Tailors, Brunswick Bldg., 69 W. Washington St., Chicago, Illinois 60602.

Vocational Guidance and Rehabilitation Service, 2239 East 55th Street, Cleveland, Ohio 44103.

Recipes for
Homemade Art Supplies

Homemade "Dough Clay"

A four-year-old can soon learn to measure and make "Dough Clay," put it in a wax paper, and store it in a cool place. Mix together two cups of flour, one cup of salt, and one teaspoonful of alum. Add ½ cupful of water, slowly. (Amount of water will depend on the consistency desired.) Color may be added by using a small amount of food coloring or powdered tempera paint.

By limiting the area where clay may be used, mothers can avoid time-consuming cleanup jobs. A breadboard makes a good base and also defines the necessary limits. Allow plenty of room so the child may stand or sit and have free use of his arms. Cookie cutters, an old spoon, plastic lids, tinfoil plates, small plastic trucks for loading and unloading, a small rolling pin or tongue depressors are fun to use.

Homemade Paste

Mix together in a dishpan one cup of laundry starch with one cup of cold water. Add two gallons of boiling water and stir until the mixture becomes transparent. When it is cool, it is ready to use.

Demonstrate to the children how they can hold the corners of a sheet of paper and draw it through the starch solution, so that both sides are covered. The sticky starch-covered sheets should be placed on a large sheet of newspaper to prevent dripping.

The dry paper with the sticky sheet attached can be placed on a child's table. Any kind of material that appeals to the child can be stuck onto the surface. Pictures and patterns can be made with such things as seeds, leaves, sticks, feathers, grains of sand, cereal, yarn, ribbon, and cotton. Material may be shifted until paste dries.

This same paste may be colored with powdered chalk and serve as a substitute for finger paint.

Homemade Finger Paint

Combine ½ cup laundry starch with one cup of cold water in a medium-size saucepan. Add 2 cups hot water and cook over medium heat until the mixture comes to a boil, stirring constantly. Remove from heat and blend in one envelope unflavored gelatin which has been soaked for five minutes in ¼ cup of cold water. Add ½ cup mild soap flakes and stir until the mixture thickens and the soap is thoroughly dissolved.

To make colored finger paint, add a tablespoonful of any kind of dye or powder paint, such as food coloring or Easter egg dye. Children have a fine time in combining colors to make new colors.

Keep finger paint in covered containers in a cool place. Plastic mustard or catsup squeeze bottles are easy to store and fun for the children to use. Regular finger paint paper may be purchased or shelf-paper which is glazed on one side can be cut to the desired size.

Water Color Paint

Buy dry powdered paint and help the child to mix his own colors. Any jar with a tight lid is good for mixing, but it should be filled only half full with equal amounts of water and dry paint. Shake well. Equal amounts of powder and water may also be mixed with an ordinary egg beater.

Some children like working on a table top, and some prefer an easel. Pour a small quantity of each color into small muffin tins or into a plastic egg tray. If the painting is done on an easel rather than a table, a thicker paint can be used. A simple easel can be made from a cardboard box by simply cutting it from corner to corner so that it forms a triangle. With an apron to protect his clothes, a flat-edged brush that is about one-half inch wide, a jar of water to clean his brush, an old sponge or paint cloth, the child is ready to go to work.

Sources of Devices

Easy-to-use gadgets and devices are to be found in a variety of places. The following are listed because of the ease in securing them by mail. In general, items required in the home care of the more severely handicapped will be found in the Rehabilitation Equipment catalogs, although mail-order houses are expanding their offerings. "Gift and gadget" houses carry a great variety of small items that may be useful in helping the person with limitations accomplish a variety of tasks. Individual manufacturers are listed when their product is not readily available elsewhere. (For addresses see Appendix H.)

Periodicals

Periodicals published by, or for, the handicapped are often an additional source of information regarding commercial or adapted equipment or devices.

Accent on Living	National Star Newsletter
Accent on Information	Paraplegia News
Achievement	Performance
Handy-Cap Horizons	Rehabilitation Gazette
International Rehabilitation Review	Rehabilitation Literature
Journal of Rehabilitation	Rehabilitation Record
NAPH Newsletter	The Squeaky Wheel
National Hookup	The Spokesman

Commercial Sources of Devices

Local

4. Local building supply company.
5. Local hardware stores.
6. Housewares department, local department stores.

Mail Order Houses (Send for catalog or obtain one through local offices.)

7. Montgomery Ward.
8. Sears, Roebuck and Company.

Jobbers and Distributors of Supplies and Equipment Used in Rehabilitation

9. J. A. Preston Corporation, 71 Fifth Avenue, South, New York, New York 10003.
10. Rehab Aids, 5913 S.W. 8th Street, Miami, Florida 33144.
11. Rehabilitation Equipment, Incorporated, 175 East 83rd Street, New York, New York 10028.
12. Rehabilitation Products, American Hospital Supply Corporation, 2020 Ridge Avenue, Evanston, Illinois 60201.
13. Scully Walton, 505 East 116th Street, New York, New York 10023.

Mail-Order Gift and Gadget Houses

14. Breck's of Boston, 100 Breck Building, Boston, Massachusetts 02210.
15. Downs and Company, 1014 Davis Street, Department 165, Evanston, Illinois 60204.
16. Hammacher Schlemmer, 145 East 57th Street, New York, New York 10022.
17. Miles Kimball, 41 West 8th Avenue, Oshkosh, Wisconsin 54901.
18. Spencer Gifts, 77R Spencer Building, Atlantic City, New Jersey 08404.
19. Sunset House, 128 Sunset Building, Beverly Hills, California 90213.

Manufacturers

20. American Standard Plumbing and Heating Division, 40 West 40th Street, New York, New York 10018.
21. Approved Products Company, 205 East 42nd Street, New York, New York 10017.
22. Black and Decker Manufacturing Company, Towson 4, Maryland.
23. Edlund Manufacturing Company, Burlington, Vermont.
24. L. H. Eubank and Son, P.O. Box 37, Inglewood, California 04956.
25. Franklin Engineering Company, New Vineyard, Maine.
26. Frigidaire, 500 East Huntington Park, Philadelphia, Pa. 19124.
27. Inclinator Company of America, 2200 Paxton Boulevard, Harrisburg, Pennsylvania 17111.
28. Mead Johnson and Company, Evansville, Indiana 47721.

29. National Steel Products Co., 1111 N. Formosa Ave., Los Angeles, California 90046.
29a. Olle Blomqvist Ingenjürsfirma, Artillerigatan 38, Stockholm, Sweden.
30. Overhead Door Corporation, Hartford City, Indiana 47348.
31. Rival Manufacturing Company, 36th and Bennington, Kansas City, Missouri 64129.
32. Rubbermaid Incorporated, Wooster, Ohio 44692.
33. Stanley Home Products, Customer Service, East Hampton, Massachusetts 01027.
34. Saf-T-Rail Company, P.O. Box 2891, St. Petersburg, Florida 33731.
35. Sunbeam Corporation, 5400 Roosevelt Road, Chicago, Illinois 60650

Additional Sources

36. Be O.K. Sales Co., Box 32, Brookfield, Illinois 60513.
37. Cleo Living Aids, 3957 Mayfield Road, Cleveland, Ohio 44121.
38. Fashion-Able, Rocky Hill, New Jersey 08553.
39. Gifts and Gadgets of Dallas, 724 South Sherman Street, Richardson, Texas 75080.
40. G. E. Miller, Inc. 484 Broadway, Yonkers, New York 10705.
41. Rehabilitation Aids, 5913 S.W. 8th Street, Box 612, Miami, Florida 33144.
42. Winco Products, Winfield Co., Inc., 3062 46th Avenue, North, St. Petersburg, Florida 33714.

Agencies and Publishers†

Abilities, Incorporated
    Albertson, New York 11507
Accent on Information
    Box 700
    Bloomington, Illinois 61701
*Accent on Living
    Box 700
    Bloomington, Illinois 61701
*Achievement
    925 N.E. 122 Street, North
    Miami, Florida 33161
ACTION
    806 Connecticut Avenue, N.W.
    Washington, D.C. 20525
Active Corps of Executives (Ace)
(See ACTION)
Administration on Aging
    U.S. Department of Health,
    Education and Welfare
    Washington, D.C. 20201
*Aging Magazine
    Administration on Aging
    Government Printing Office
    Washington, D.C. 20402
Alcoholics Anonymous
    Box 459 Grand Central Station
    New York, New York 10017
American Automobile Association
    1712 G Street, N.W.
    Washington, D.C. 20006
American Association for Health,
Physical Education and Recreation
Program for the Handicapped
    1201 16th Street, N.W.
    Washington, D.C. 20036

(American Assoc. of Retired
    Persons and National Retired
    Teachers Association
    National Headquarters
    1909 K Street, N.W.
    Washington, D.C. 20006
American Cancer Society
    219 East 42nd Street
    New York, New York 10017
American Dental Association
    Bureau of Dental Health
    Education
    211 East Chicago Avenue
    Chicago, Illinois 60611
American Diabetes Association
    18 East 48th Street
    New York, New York 10017
American Dietetic Association
    620 North Michigan Avenue
    Chicago, Illinois 60611
American Foundation for the Blind
    15 West 16th Street
    New York, New York 10011
American Heart Association
    44 East 23rd Street
    New York, New York 10010
American Home Economics
Association
    2010 Massachusetts Ave., N.W.
    Washington, D.C. 20036
American Institute of Architects
    1735 New York Avenue, N.W.
    Washington, D.C. 20006
American Library Association
    50 East Huron Street
    Chicago, Illinois 60611

*Asterisk indicates magazine or newsletter.
†(Referred to in the text or in the bibliography).

American Lung Association
1740 Broadway
New York, New York 10019
American Medical Association
535 North Dearborn Street
Chicago, Illinois 60610
American Museum of Natural
History
Central Park West at 79th Street
New York, New York 10024
American Occupational Therapy
Association
6000 Executive Blvd.
Rockville, Maryland 20852
American Optometric Association
Public Information Division
P.O. Box 13157
St. Louis, Missouri 63119
American Physical Therapy
Association
1156 15th Street, N.W.
Washington, D.C. 20005
American Podiatry Association
20 Chevy Chase Circle, N.W.
Washington, D.C. 20015
American Red Cross
National Headquarters
17th and D Streets, N.W.
Washington, D.C. 20006
American Rehabilitation
Foundation
1800 Chicago Avenue
Minneapolis, Minnesota 55404
American Society of Landscape
Architects Foundation
1750 Old Meadows Road
McLean, Virginia 22101
American Speech and Hearing
Association
9030 Old Georgetown Road
Washington, D.C. 20014
American Standards Association
10 East 40th Street
New York, New York 10016

Arkansas Rehabilitation Service
Hot Springs Rehabilitation
Center
Hot Springs, Arkansas 71901
The Arthritis Foundation
1212 Avenue of the Americas
New York, New York 10036
Association for Children with
Learning Disabilities
2200 Brownsville Road
Pittsburgh, Pennsylvania 15210
Australian Council for
Rehabilitation of Disabled
Cleaveland House
Cor. Bedford & Buckingham
Streets
Sydney 2000, Australia
Boy Scouts of America
New Brunswick, New Jersey
08903
Bridge Travel Service
832 East Atlantic Avenue
Delray Beach, Florida 33444
Bureau of Outdoor Recreation
U.S. Department of the Interior
Washington, D.C. 20240
Camp Fire Girls, Inc.
1740 Broadway
New York, New York 10019
Canadian Arthritis and
Rheumatism Society
900 Yonge Street
Toronto 5, Ontario, Canada
Canadian Rehabilitation Council
for the Disabled
242 St. George Street
Toronto 5, Ontario, Canada
Center of Leisure Studies
University of Oregon
1587 Agate Street
Eugene, Oregon 97403
Central Council for the Disabled
34 Eccleston Square
London, S.W.1, England

Child Life Play Specialties
Equipment for Active Indoor and
Outdoor Use
  55 Whitney Street
  Holliston, Massachusetts 01746
Child Study Association of America
  9 East 89th Street
  New York, New York 10003
  Denver, Colorado 80216
  67 Irving Place
  New York, New York 10003
Clothing and Research
Development Foundation, Inc.
  48 East 66th Street
  New York, New York 10021
Child Welfare League of America
Colorado Division of Game,
Fish and Parks
  6060 North Broadway
Colorado State University
  College of Home Economics
  Fort Collins, Colorado 80521
Connecticut Agricultural
Experiment Station
  University of Connecticut
  Storrs, Connecticut 06268
Consumer Product Information
  Public Documents Distribution
  Center
  Pueblo, Colorado 81009
Cornell University
Housing Research Center
  College of Human Ecology
  Ithaca, New York 14850
Council of Better Business Bureaus
  1150 17th Street, N.W.
  Washington, D.C. 20036
Council for Exceptional Children
  1411 S. Jefferson Davis Highway
  Arlington, Virginia 22202
Danish National Association for
Infantile Paralysis
Testing and Observation Institute
  Tubergvej 5, D.K. 2900
  Hellerup, Denmark

Disabled Living Foundation
  346 High Street
  Kensington
  London, W.14, 8 N.S., England
Disabled Veterans of America
  P.O. Box 4301
  Cincinnati, Ohio 45201
Everest & Jennings, Inc.
  1803 Pontius Avenue
  Los Angeles, California 90025
Evergreen Travel Service
  19429 44th Avenue W.
  Lynwood, Washington 98036
*Family Health Magazine
  1271 Avenue of the Americas
  New York, New York 10020
Family Service Association of
America
  44 East 23rd Street
  New York, New York 10010
Fashion-Able
  Rocky Hill, New Jersey 08553
Federation of the Handicapped
  211 West 14th Street
  New York, New York 10011
Finnish Association of Disabled
Civilians and Service Men
  Mannerheimintie 44A
  Helsinki, Finland
Finnish Committee I.S.R.D.
  Insurance Rehabilitation Agency
  Pohjoinen Rautatiekatu 23 B
  00100 Helsinki 10 Finland
Florida State University
Department of Urban and
Rural Planning
  Tallahassee, Florida 32306
Folksam Insurance Company
  Stockholm, Sweden
Foster Grandparent Program
(F.G.P.)
  (See ACTION)
Food and Drug Administration
  Office of Consumer Affairs
  5600 Fishers Lane
  Rockville, Maryland 20852

4-H Clubs
Agricultural Extension Service
  U.S. Dept. of Agriculture
  Washington, D.C. 20250
Girl Scouts of the United States
of America
  830 Third Avenue
  New York, New York 10022
Governor's Committee on
Employment of the Handicapped
  (Address your state capital)
Georgia State Department of Parks
  270 Washington Street, S.W.
  Atlanta, Georgia 30334
Handicap Village, Inc.
  1200 North Ninth Street
  Clear Lake, Iowa 50428
*Handy-Cap Horizons
  3250 E. Loretta Drive
  Indianapolis, Indiana 46227
*Harvest Years
  Harvest Years Publishing Co.
  104 East 40th Street
  New York, New York 10016
Hofstra University
  Hempstead, New York 11550
Home Economics Extension
Division
  U.S. Department of Agriculture
  Washington, D.C. 20250
  (Write your State Land Grant
  University)
Homemaker Services
  (Contact local Social Welfare
  Office)
  (See also National Council
  Homemaker-Health Aides)
Home Study Courses
  (Write your State University and
  your local Board of Education)
Human Resources Center
  Albertson, Long Island
  New York 11507
Indoor Sports Club, Inc.
  732 E. Draper Street
  Mesa, Arizona 85203

Institute of Life Insurance
  277 Park Avenue
  New York, New York 10017
Institute of Lifetime Learning
  Dupont Circle Building
  1346 Connecticut Avenue, N.W.
  Washington, D.C. 20036
Institute of Rehabilitation
Medicine
  Learning and Resources Facility
  New York University Medical
  Center
  400 East 34th Street
  New York, New York 10016
Interior Designers
  National Headquarters
  315 East 62nd Street
  New York, New York 10021
International Association of
Rehabilitation Facilities
  5530 Wisconsin Avenue
  Suite 955
  Washington, D.C. 20015
*I.C.R.A. News Letter
  Information Center
  Recreation for the Handicapped
  Southern Illinois University
  Carbondale, Illinois 62901
*I.C.T.A. Information Center
  International Committee on
  Technical Aids
  Fack S-161-03
  Bromma 3, Sweden
International Film Bureau, Inc.
  332 S. Michigan Avenue
  Chicago, Illinois 60604
*International Rehabilitation
Review
  219 East 44th Street
  New York, New York 10017
International Senior Citizens
Association, Inc.
  17753 Wilshire Blvd.
  Los Angeles, California 90024
Invaliidisäätiö
  Tenholantie 10
  Helsinki, Finland

Jon Dol & Associates
Vertical Gardening Equipment
17602 Queens Wreath
Irvine, California 92664
*Journal of Home Economics
2010 Massachusetts Avenue,
N.W.
Washington, D.C. 20036
*Journal of Occupational Therapy
6000 Executive Blvd.
Rockville, Md. 20852
*Journal of Rehabilitation
1522 K Street, N.W.
Washington, D.C. 20005
*Journal of Rehabilitation in Asia
The Amerind 15th Road,
Khar Bombay, 52 India
Judd's Travel Headquarters
148 West Bridge Street—Box 382
Owatonna, Minnesota 55060
Kenny Rehabilitation Institute
1800 Chicago Avenue
Minneapolis, Minnesota 55404
Kidney Disease Control Program
5600 Fishers Lane
Rockville, Maryland 20852
Kings College Hospital
London, S.E. 5, England
Leinenweber, Inc., Custom Tailors
69 W. Washington Street
Chicago, Illinois 60602
The Library of Congress
Division For the Blind and
Physically Handicapped
Washington, D.C. 20542
Massachusetts Home Economics
Association
Skinner Hall
University of Massachusetts
Amherst, Massachusetts 01002
Maternal and Child Health
Services
U.S. Public Health Service
Rockville, Maryland 20852

Michigan State University
College of Human Ecology
East Lansing, Michigan 48823
Michigan-Wayne State
Institute of Gerontology
1021 E. Huron Street
Ann Arbor, Michigan 48104
(Also write your State
University)
Minnesota Society for Crippled
Children and Adults
2004 Lyndale Avenue, South
Minneapolis, Minnesota 55405
*Modern Maturity
215 Long Beach Blvd.
Long Beach, California 90801
Mobile Home Manufacturing
Association
Consumer Education Division
14650 Lee Road—Box 201
Chantilly, Virginia 22021
Muscular Dystrophy Association
of America, Inc.
1790 Broadway
New York, New York 10019
National Association of Housing
and Redevelopment Officials
2600 Virginia Avenue N.W.
Washington, D.C. 20037
National Association for Mental
Health
800 N. Kent Street
Rosslyn, Virginia 22209
National Association of the
Physically Handicapped
2 Meetinghouse Road
Merrimack, New Hampshire
03054
National Association of Social
Workers
600 Southern Building
15th and H Street, N.W.
Washington, D.C. 20005
National Audiovisual Center
Washington, D.C. 20409

National Audubon Society
  950 Third Avenue
  New York, New York 10022
National Cancer Institute
  Bethesda, Maryland 20014
National Center for Health
Statistics
  Public Health Service
  H.S.M.H.A.
  Rockville, Maryland 20852
National Center for Voluntary
Action
  1735 Eye Street, N.W.
  Washington, D.C. 20006
National Clearinghouse for
Alcohol Information
  (N.C.A.L.I.) Box 2345
  Rockville, Maryland 20852
National Commission on
Architectural Barriers for
Rehabilitation of the Handicapped
  Social and Rehabilitation Service
  Washington, D.C. 20210
National Congress of Organizations
of Physically Handicapped
  7611 Oakland Avenue
  Minneapolis, Minnesota 55423
National Coordinating Council on
Drug Abuse Education
and Information
  Box 19400
  Washington, D.C. 20036
National Council on the Aging
  1828 L Street, N.W.
  Washington, D.C. 20036
National Council on Family
Relations
  1219 University Avenue
  Southeast
  Minneapolis, Minnesota 55414
National Council for Homemaker-
Home Health Aide Services, Inc.
  67 Irving Place
  New York, New York 10003
National Council for Senior
Citizens
  1627 K Street, N.W.
  Washington, D.C. 20006

National Easter Seal Society for
Crippled Children and Adults
  2023 West Ogden Avenue
  Chicago, Illinois 60612
National Foundation—March
of Dimes
  Box 2000
  White Plains, New York 10602
National Fund for Research into
Poliomyelitis and Other
Crippling Diseases
  Vincent House, Vincent Square
  London, S.W.1, England
National Hearing Aid Society
  24261 Grand River Avenue
  Detroit, Michigan 48219
National Heart and Lung Institute
  Bethesda, Maryland 20014
National Home Study Council
  1601 18th Street, N.W.
  Washington, D.C. 20009
*National Hookup
  0536 Mason Street
  Riverside, California 92503
National Institute of Arthritis
and Metabolic Diseases
  Bethesda, Maryland 20014
National Institute of Health
  Bethesda, Maryland 20014
National Institute of Mental
Health
  5600 Fishers Lane
  Rockville, Maryland 20852
National League for Nursing
  10 Columbus Circle
  New York, New York 10019
National League of Cities
  1612 K Street, N.W.
  Washington, D.C. 20006
National Medical Audiovisual
Center
  National Library of Medicine
  Annex—Station K
  Atlanta, Georgia 30324
National Multiple Sclerosis Society
  257 Park Avenue, South
  New York, New York 10017

National Odd Shoe Exchange
1415 Ocean Front
Santa Monica, California 90401
National Paraplegia Foundation
333 North Michigan Avenue
Chicago, Illinois 60601
National Park Service
Department of the Interior
Washington, D.C. 20240
(Also consult your State Park
Service)
National Recreation and Parks
Association
1601 North Kent Street
Arlington, Virginia 22209
National Rehabilitation
Association
1522 K Street, N.W.
Washington, D.C. 20005
National Retired Teachers
Association
(See A.A.R.P.)
National Safety Council
Dept. H.P.O. Box 11171
Chicago, Illinois 60611
National Senior Citizens
Law Center
942 Market Street—Suite 606
San Francisco, California 94102
National Society of Interior
Designers
315 E. 62nd Street
New York, New York 10021
National Society For the
Prevention of Blindness
79 Madison Avenue
New York, New York 10016
*National Star Newsletter
6219 Naper Avenue
Chicago, Illinois 60631
National Trails Council
c/o Open Lands Project
53 West Jackson Blvd.
Chicago, Illinois 60604

National Therapeutic Recreation
Society
National Recreation and
Parks Association
1601 North Kent Street
Arlington, Virginia 22209
National Voluntary Organizations
For Services to Older People
Administration on Aging
Washington, D.C. 20201
National Wheelchair Athletic
Association
40–24 62nd Street
Woodside, New York 11377
Netherlands Central Society for
the Care of the Disabled
Stadhouderslaan 142
The Hague, Netherlands
New York University
Construction Fund
194 Washington Avenue
Albany, New York 12210
North America Riding for the
Handicapped Assoc., Inc.
Mrs. Octavia J. Brown
Editor, News Letter
Cokesbury Road R D.
Annandale, New Jersey 08801
North Dakota State University
Agricultural Information
Fargo, North Dakota 58102
Nutrition Foundation
99 Park Avenue
New York, New York 10016
Office of Consumer Services
U.S. Department of Health,
Education and Welfare
Washington, D.C. 20201
*Paraplegia News
935 Coastline Drive
Seal Beach, California 90740
Paralyzed Veterans of America,
Inc.
3636 Sixteenth Street, N.W.
Washington, D.C. 20010
Peace Corps (See ACTION)

Pennsylvania State University
College of Human Development
University Park, Pennsylvania
16802
*Performance
President's Committee on
Employment of the
Handicapped
Washington, D.C. 20201
*Physical Therapy Review
1156 15th Street, N.W.
Washington, D.C. 20005
Planned Parenthood—
World Population
810 7th Avenue
New York, New York 10019
*President's Committee on
Employment of the Handicapped
(Newsletter Committee on
Recreation and Leisure; also,
Newsletter Committee on
Barrier Free Design)
Washington, D.C. 20210
President's Committee on
Mental Retardation
Washington, D.C. 20201
Public Affairs Pamphlets
481 Park Avenue
New York, New York 10016
Public Health Service
Division of Chronic Diseases
U.S. Department of Health,
Education and Welfare
Washington, D.C. 20201
Public Housing Administration
Housing and Home Finance
Agency
Washington, D.C. 20413
Recreation Center for the
Handicapped
Fleischbacker near Sloat Blvd.
San Francisco, California 94132
*Rehabilitation
British Council for
Rehabilitation of the Disabled
Tavistock House South
London, WCIH, 9 L B, England

*Rehabilitation Digest
(See Canadian Rehabilitation
Council)
*Rehabilitation Gazette
4502 Maryland Avenue
St. Louis, Missouri 63108
Rehabilitation International,
U.S.A.
219 East 44th Street
New York, New York 10017
*Rehabilitation Literature
2023 West Ogden Avenue
Chicago, Illinois 60612
*Rehabilitation Psychology
Box 26034
Tempe, Arizona 85282
*Rehabilitation Record
Rehabilitation Services
Administration
Washington, D.C. 20201
Rehabilitation Services
Administration
U.S. Department of Health,
Education and Welfare
Washington, D.C. 20402
Retired Senior Volunteer Program
(R.S.V.P.)
(See ACTION)
Royal Institute of British
Architects
66 Portland Place
London, W. 1, England
Scottish Housing Advisory
Committee
Her Majesty's Stationery Office
Edinburgh, Scotland
Senior Citizen Service
Organizations
(See local telephone directory)
Service Corps of Retired
Executives (SCORE)
(See ACTION)
SIECUS (Sex Information and
Education Council)
1855 Broadway
New York, New York 10023

Ski Touring Council
    West Hill Road
    Troy, Vermont 05868
Small Homes Council
    University of Illinois
    Urbana, Illinois 61803
*Snow Sports
    1500 East 79th Street
    Minneapolis, Minnesota 55420
Social and Rehabilitation Services
    U.S. Department of Health,
    Education and Welfare
    Mary E. Switzer Memorial
    Building
    Washington, D.C. 20201
Social Security Administration
    Baltimore, Maryland 21235
Social Services and Welfare
Organizations
    (See local telephone directory)
Society and Home for the Disabled
    Esplanaden 34
    1263 Copenhagen K, Denmark
*The Spokesman
    Western Disabled Alliance, Inc.
    Box 444
    San Lorenzo, California 94580
*The "Squeaky Wheel"
    (See National Paraplegia
    Foundation)
Superintendent of Documents
    Government Printing Office
    Washington, D.C. 20402
Swedish Central Committee
for Rehabilitation
    Fack S-161 03
    Bromma 3, Sweden
*Talking Book Topics
    (See Library of Congress)
*Therapeutic Recreation Journal
    1601 North Kent Street
    Arlington, Virginia 22209
United Cerebral Palsy Association
    66 East 34th Street
    New York, New York 10016
United Ostomy Association, Inc.
    1111 Wilshire Blvd.
    Los Angeles, California 90017

University of Alabama
    Continuing Education in
    Home Economics
    Box 2987
    University, Alabama 35486
University of Cincinnati
Medical Center
    Department of Physical
    Medicine and Rehabilitation
    234 Goodman Street
    Cincinnati, Ohio 45229
University of Connecticut
    Audio-Visual Center
    Storrs, Connecticut 06268
University of Connecticut
    School of Home Economics
    Storrs, Connecticut 06268
University of Illinois
    Department of Home
    Economics
    Urbana, Illinois 61803
University of Illinois
    Student Rehabilitation Center
    Urbana, Illinois 61801
University of Missouri
    Services to the Handicapped
    Columbia, Missouri 65201
University of Nebraska
    College of Home Economics
    Extension Service
    Lincoln, Nebraska 68503
University of Vermont
    Department of Home
    Economics
    Burlington, Vermont 05401
Urban Mass Transportation
Administration
    Office of Public Affairs
    400 7th Street, S.W.
    Washington, D.C. 20590
U.S. Department of Agriculture
    Office of Information
    Washington, D.C. 20250
U.S. Department of Housing and
Urban Development
    Washington, D.C. 20410

U.S. Department of Labor
Manpower Administration
Washington, D.C. 20210
(See also local and state offices)
U.S. Government Printing Office
Washington, D.C. 20402
U.S. Office of Education
Division on Handicapped
Children
Washington, D.C. 20202
U.S. Public Health Service
Office of Information
5600 Fishers Lane
Rockville, Maryland 20852
U.S. Social Security Administration
Division of Disability Operations
6401 Security Blvd.
Baltimore, Maryland 21235
U.S.D.A. Forest Service
Washington, D.C. 20250
Veterans Administration
Director, Voluntary Service
Washington, D.C. 20420
Veterans Administration
Information Service (064)
Washington, D.C. 20420
VISTA
(See ACTION)
Vocational Guidance and
Rehabilitation Service
2239 East 55th Street
Cleveland, Ohio 44103
Volunteers for International
Technical Assistance (VITA)
College Campus
Schenectady, New York 12308
Wayne State University
Department of Home
Economics
Detroit, Michigan 48202
Westchester County Easter Seal
Society
713 County Office Building
White Plains, New York 10601
Whitney Library of Design
130 East 59th Street
New York, New York 10022

Women's Bureau
U.S. Department of Labor
Washington, D.C. 20210
Young Men's Christian Association
National Council
219 Broadway
New York, New York 10007
Young Women's Christian
Association
National Board
600 Lexington Avenue
New York, New York 10022

Recent Additions

Iowa State University
Home Economics Extension
Service
Ames, Iowa 50010
International Federation on Aging
1909 K Street, N.W.
Washington, D.C. 20006
*New York Times—Large Type Ed.
Box 1227
Flushing, N.Y. 11352
*Human Needs
Social and Rehabilitation Services
Dept. Health, Education and
Welfare
Washington, D.C. 20201
People to People Program
1146 16th Street, N.W.
Washington, D.C. 20036
*Readers Digest Editor
Large-Type Edition, Braille
and Talking Records
Pleasantville, New York 10570

Bibliography and Sources
of Teaching Materials

Space permits the listing of only a few references of value to homemakers and their families and to professional personnel concerned with rehabilitation. Additional references are included in the bibliographies in the publications listed. Addresses of publishers are listed alphabetically in Appendix H. (See also Bibliography Supplement, Page 238)

Clothing

1. Bare, Clari; Boettke, Eleanor, and Waggoner, Neva, *Self-Help Clothing for Handicapped Children.* Chicago: National Society for Crippled Children and Adults, 1962.
2. Bergh, Marie, *Clothing for the Handicapped.* 4 pp. Oslo: Norwegian Rheumatism Society, Norsk Revmatiker Forbund, Professor Dahlgate 32, Oslo, 2, Norway, 1965.
3. Boettke, Eleanor, *Suggestions for Physically Handicapped Mothers on Clothing for Pre-School Children.* Storrs: School of Home Economics, University of Connecticut, 1957.
4. Buttrup, Ellen, *Hensigtsmaessigt Toj Til Handicappede.* 32 pp. Copenhagen: Orthopedic Hospital, Hans Knudsen Plads 3, Copenhagen, Denmark, 1965.
5. Chambers, Helen G., and Moulton, Verna, *Clothing Selection—Fashions, Figure, Fabrics.* Philadelphia: J. B. Lippincott Company, Revised 1969.
6. Cookman, Helen, and Zimmerman, Muriel E., O.T.R., *Functional Fashions for the Physically Handicapped.* New York: Institute of Physical Medicine and Rehabilitation, New York University Medical Center, 1961.
7. Scott, Clarice L., *Clothes for the Physically Handicapped Homemaker.* Washington, D.C.: Clothing and Housing Research Report No. 12, 28 pp. Illustrated, 1960.

Family Relations and Child Care

8. American Home Economics Associations. List of films on *Family Relations and Child Development.* Washington, D.C.

9. Child Study Association of America. New York: Bibliography of *Books of the Year*.

10. Children's Bureau, U.S. Department of Health, Education, and Welfare. *Infant Care*. Children's Bureau Publication No. 8, 1963.

11. _____ *Your Child from One to Six*. Children's Bureau Publication No. 30, 1962.

12. Gilbreth, Lillian M., *Living with Our Children*. 254 pp. New York: W. W. Norton and Company, Inc., 1951.

13. Grinstein, Alexander, and Sterba, Editha, *Understanding Your Family*. Bibliography. New York: Random House, 1957.

14. Jenkins, Gladys G., Shacter, Helen, and Bauer, William W., *These Are Your Children*, 320 pp. Illustrated. Annotated bibliography. Chicago: Scott, Foresman and Company, 1953.

15. Levy, J., and Munroe, R., *The Happy Family*. New York: Alfred A. Knopf, Inc., 1938.

16. May, Elizabeth E., and Waggoner, Neva R., *Work Simplification in the Area of Child Care*. 32 pp. School of Home Economics, University of Connecticut, and the Office of Vocational Rehabilitation, 1962.

17. Nolan, Francena L., *Helping Michael to Help Himself*. Extension Bulletin 834. Ithaca: Cornell University, May, 1955.

18. Public Affairs Pamphlets. Catalog available on request.

19. Science Research Associates. Catalog of pamphlets on request.

20. Spock, B., *Common Sense Book of Baby and Child Care*. New York: Duell, Sloan, and Pearce, Inc., 1954. Pocket Book Edition: *Baby and Child Care*. 502 pp. New York: Pocket Books, Inc., 1957.

21. Waggoner, Neva R., and Reedy, Garland W., *Child Care Equipment for Physically Handicapped Mothers*. 38 pp. Illustrated. Storrs: School of Home Economics, University of Connecticut, 1959.

22. Wall, Jessie, *Play Experiences Handicapped Mothers May Share with Young Children*. Illustrated. Storrs: School of Home Economics, University of Connecticut, 1960.

Homes and Furnishings

23. American Standards Association, *Making Buildings and Facilities Accessible to, and Usable by, the Physically Handicapped*. 12 pp. New York: 1961. National Society for Crippled Children and Adults.

24. Diamond, Beverly, Editor, *Furniture Requirements for Older People*. 46 pp. Bibliography. New York: National Council on the Aging.

25. *Elevators and Ramps*. Illustrated. Planographed. Spiral binding. Detroit: We, the Handicapped, Inc., 1957.

26. Goldsmith, Selwyn, *Designing for the Disabled*. Technical Information Service of the Royal Institute of British Architects, 1963.

27. Howard, Mildred S., and Parker, W. Russell, *Planning Bathrooms for Today's Homes*. 20 pp. Illustrated. Home and Garden Bulletin No. 99. Washington, D.C.: U.S. Department of Agriculture, November, 1964.

28. ––– *Housing for the Elderly*. A.R.S. 63-1. 22 pp. Washington, D.C.: Housing and Clothing Research Division, U.S. Department of Agriculture, 1963.

29. Judson, Julia S., Wagner, Elizabeth, and Zimmerman, Muriel E., *Homemaking and Housing for the Disabled in the United States of America*. 80 pp. Rehabilitation Monograph XX. New York: The Institute of Physical Medicine and Rehabilitation, 1962.
30. Leschly, Vibeke; Kjaer, Alice, and Kjaer, Borge, *General Lines in Designs of Dwellings for Handicapped Confined to Wheelchairs, Part I*, 66 pp. Denmark: Danish National Assocaition for Infantile Paralysis, Testing and Observation Institute, 1959.
31. McGuire, Marie C., *Architect's Check List*. 16 pp. Washington, D.C.: Public Housing Administration, Housing and Home Finance Agency, 1962.
32. Musson, Noverre, and Heusinkyeld, Helen, *Buildings for the Elderly*. 216 pp. New York: Reinhold, 1963.
33. National Society for Crippled Children and Adults, *Survey Blanks for Making a Community Guide of Buildings and Facilities Accessible to the Handicapped*. Single copies free.
33a. *Bibliography on Housing for the Handicapped*.
34. Netherlands Central Society for the Care of Disabled, *Housing for the Disabled*. 48 pp. Illustrated. Bibliography. New York: International Society for the Rehabilitation of the Disabled, 1958.
35. Nugent, Timothy J., *Design of Buildings to Permit Their Use by the Physically Handicapped*. Publication #910. 16 pp. Illustrated. New Building Research, President's Committee for the Employment of the Handicapped. Fall, 1960.
36. President's Council on Aging, *Ideas for Americans* from Homes for the Aged in Sweden. Washington, D.C.: U.S. Government Printing Office, 1963.
37. Rusk, Howard A., Lawton, Edith B., Elvin, Faith; Judson, Julia, and Zimmerman, Muriel, *The Functional Home for Easier Living*. 16 pp. Illustrated. Bibliography. New York: Institute of Physical Medicine and Rehabilitation, 1960.
38. Steinberg, H. A., *A Check List for Retirement Homes*. Urbana: Small Homes Council, University of Illinois, 1958.
39. Wagner, Elizabeth, and Zimmerman, Muriel E., *Approaches to Independent Living*. Manual IV of Study Courses in Occupational Therapy, 72 pp. Dubuque: William C. Brown Company, Publishers, 1962.
40. Paralyzed Veterans of America, *Wheelchair Houses*. 16 pp. Illustrated. Swissdale, Pennsylvania: 1961.
41. American Heart Association, *Do It Yourself Again*. New York: American Heart Association, 1965.
42. Agerholm, Margaret; Hollings, Elizabeth M., and Williams, Wanda M., *Equipment for the Disabled: An Index of Aids and Ideas for the Disabled*. 4 vols. Looseleaf. London, England: National Fund for Research into Poliomyelitis and Other Crippling Diseases, 1961.
43. Australian Red Cross Society, New South Wales Division, and the Australian Council for Rehabilitation of Aids for the Disabled, *Report on the Exhibition of Aids for the Disabled*. 32 pp. 1958.
44. Invaliidisäätiö (Invalid Hospital), *Apunevwoja—Invalidiper Enemnille*. (Suggestion for Disabled Homemaker.) 16 pp. Helsinki, Finland, 1961.

45. Lowman, Edward W., and Rusk, Howard A., *The Helping Hand: Self-Help Devices.* 18 pp. Illustrated. New York: Institute of Physical Medicine and Rehabilitation and Arthritis Self-Help Device Office, 1963.
46. Moore, Josephine C., O.T.R., *Rehabilitation Equipment and Supplies Directory.* Michigan: Overbeck Bookstore.
47. New York University, Bellevue Medical Center Institute of Physical Medicine and Rehabilitation, and the National Foundation, *Self-Help Devices for Rehabilitation.* 418 pp. Illustrated. Dubuque: William C. Brown Company, 1958.
48. Public Health Service, Division of Chronic Diseases, *Up and Around.* Washington, D.C.: U.S. Government Printing Office, 1964.
49. Steinke, Norma, and Erickson, Patricia, *Homemaking Aids for the Disabled.* 15 pp. Illustrated. Bibliography. Minneapolis: Kenny Rehabilitation Institute, 1963.

Home Management with Emphasis on Work Simplification

50. American Heart Association, *The Heart of the Home.* 28 pp. New York: 1956.
51. Bevacqua, Katherine M., Gerhold, Marilyn O., and Ruef, Ruth H., *Sewing and House Cleaning Units for Cardiac Homemakers.* Publication #175. 24 pp. Illustrated. Bibliography. University Park, Pennsylvania: College of Home Economics, June, 1960.
52. Central Committee for the Welfare of Cripples in Sweden, *The Physically Handicapped Housewife.* S.V.K.C.'s Publication Series No. 6. 68 pp. Illustrated. 1959.
53. Fish, H. U., *Take It Easy.* Seattle: Washington State Heart Association, 1961.
54. Grady, E. R., *Body Mechanics in Homemaking Tasks.* Kingston: University of Rhode Island, College of Home Economics, January, 1954.
55. Gilbreth, Lilliam M., Thomas, Orpha M., and Clymer, Eleanor, *Management in the Home.* 293 pp. New York: Dodd, Mead and Company, 1959.
56. Gross, Irma H., and Crandall, Elizabeth W., *Management for Modern Families.* 589 pp. New York: Appleton-Century-Crofts, 1963.
57. Laclede Gas Company, Home Service Department, *Helpful Homemaking Hints.* St. Louis, Missouri.
58. Johnston, Betty Jane, *Equipment for Modern Living.* New York: Macmillan Company, 1965.
59. Kettunen, R. C., *Take It Easy.* (Four pamphlets.) East Lansing: Michigan State University, Cooperative Extension Service, 1956.
60. National Tuberculosis Association, *Homemaking Hints.* 24 pp. New York: 1954.
61. Nickell, P., and Dorsey, J. M., *Management in Family Living.* 551 pp. Third Edition. New York: John Wiley and Sons, Inc., 1959.
62. Richardson, M., and McCracken, E. C., *Energy Expenditures of Women Performing Selected Activities.* Washington, D.C.: Home Economics Service, U.S. Department of Agriculture, December, 1960.
63. Rusk, Howard A., Kristeller, Edith L., Judson, Julia, Hunt, Gladys, and Zimmerman, Muriel, *A Manual for Training the Disabled Homemaker.* Second edition. Rehabilitation Monograph VIII, 167 pp. Illustrated. Bibliography, 1961.

64. Sanderson, F., and Pretzer, H., *Easy Does It.* (Six leaflets.) Detroit: Wayne State University, 1954.
65. Wright, Russell and Mary, *Guide to Easier Living.* 201 pp. New York: Simon and Schuster, 1954.
66. Zmola, Gertrude M., *You Can Do Family Laundry with Hand Limitations.* 16 pp. Storrs: School of Home Economics, University of Connecticut, 1959.

Home Safety

67. Harper, G. W., Florio, A. E., and Stafford, G. T., *Hazard-Free Houses for All.* Circular Series Cl. 1, 8 pp. Urbana: Small Homes Council, 1958.
68. National Safety Council, Home Safety Department. List of publications available.
69. National Society for Crippled Children and Adults, *Safety Check List for the Aging and the Handicapped* and *Safety Check List for Parents—Is Your Child Safe?* List of publications available.
70. Waldschmidt, P., and Sanderson, F. G., *Home Wiring for the Physically Limited.* Pittsburgh: National Electric Products.

Kitchen Planning

71. Berg, Ing-Marie, and Muller, Hendrick, *Kitchen for Disabled Homemakers.* Ni 1. Stockholm, Sweden: National Institute for Consumer Education, 1951.
72. Howard, Mildred S., Thye, L. S., and Tayloe, G. K., *The Beltsville Kitchen-Workroom with Energy-Saving Features.* 13 pp. Home and Garden Bulletin #60. Washington, D.C.: U.S. Department of Agriculture, November, 1958.
73. Howard, Mildred S., Thye, L. S., and Parker, W. B., *Beltsville Energy-Saving Kitchen Design No. 2.* Leaflet #463. 4 pp. Washington, D.C.: U.S. Department of Agriculture, November, 1959.
74. Howard, Mildred S., Tayloe, G. K., and Parker, W. B., *Beltsville Energy-Saving Kitchen Design No. 3.* Leaflet #518. 8 pp. Washington, D.C.: U.S. Department of Agriculture, Clothing and Housing Research, February, 1963.
75. Howard, Mildred S., Tayloe, G. K., and Parker, W. B., *Parallel-Wall Kitchen Arrangements.* 4 pp. Miscellaneous publication No. 936. Washington, D.C.: U.S. Department of Agriculture, Clothing and Housing Research, June, 1963.
76. ——— *L-Shaped Kitchen Arrangements.* 4 pp. Miscellaneous publication No. 936. June, 1963.
77. ——— *Broken-U Kitchen Arrangements.* 4 pp. Miscellaneous publication No. 934. June, 1963.
78. ——— *U-Shaped Kitchen Arrangements.* 4 pp. Miscellaneous publication No. 933. June, 1963.
79. ——— *Corner Storage in Kitchens.* 4 pp. Miscellaneous publication No. 944. September, 1963.
80. Leschly, Vibeke; Kjaer, Alice, and Kjaer, Borge, *General Lines in Designs of Dwellings for Handicapped Confined to Wheelchairs, Part 2.* 67 pp. Hellerup, Denmark: The Testing and Observation Institute of the Danish National Association for Infantile Paralysis, 1960.
81. McCullough, Helen E., and Farnham, Mary B., *Space and Design Requirements for Wheelchair Kitchens.* 47 pp. Bulletin #661. Urbana: University of Illinois. June, 1960.

82. ——— *Kitchens for Women in Wheelchairs.* 31 pp. Circular #841. Urbana: University of Illinois. November, 1961.
83. Wheeler, Virginia Hart, *Planning Kitchens for Handicapped Homemakers.* Rehabilitation Monograph XXVII, New York: The Institute of Physical Medicine and Rehabilitation, 1965.

Nutrition

Bibliographies are available from the following sources:
84. American Heart Association
85. American Diabetes Association
86. American Dietetic Association
87. Children's Bureau, Department of Health, Education, and Welfare.
88. Home Economics Division, U.S. Department of Agriculture
89. Nutrition Foundation, Inc.
90. Nutrition Services in the Department of Health in your own state.

Personal Adjustment to a Disability

91. Ayrault, E. W., *Take One Step.* 310 pp. New York: Doubleday and Company, 1963.
92. Miers, Earl Schenck, *"Why Did This Have to Happen?"* Parents Series No. 1. 28 pp. Chicago: National Society for Crippled Children and Adults, 1957.
93. National Society for Crippled Children and Adults, *Recent Books About Handicapped Persons.* Bibliography.
94. Speare, Elizabeth G., "Where There's a Will." 18 pp. Storrs: School of Home Economics, University of Connecticut, 1959.
95. Viscardi, Henry, Jr., *A Man's Stature.* 240 pp. New York: The John Day Company, 1952. (Write for other titles by author.)
96. Wright, Beatrice A., *Physical Disability—A Psychological Approach.* Bibliography. New York: Harper and Brothers, 1960.

Recreation and Creative Activities for Children and Adults

97. American Museum of Natural History. List of publications available.
98. Farina, A. M., Smith, J. M., and Furth, S. H., *Growth Through Play.* Englewood Cliffs: Prentice-Hall, Inc., 1959.
99. Lowenfeld, V., *Your Child and His Art: A Guide for Parents.* New York: Macmillan Company, 1954. Reprinted, 1960.
100. National Audubon Society. List of publications available.
101. National Recreation Association. Consulting service on Recreation for the Ill and the Handicapped. Bibliography and list of publications available.
102. Parker, Bertha Morris, *Garden Indoors.* 36 pp. New York: Row, Peterson and Company. Basic Science Education Series—A Row-Peterson Unitext (Intermediate). 1944.
103. Pomeroy, Janet, *Recreation for the Physically Handicapped.* 382 pp. New York: Macmillan Company, 1964.

104. Turtox Service Leaflets. Chicago General Biological Supply House. Catalog available.

Rehabilitation Miscellaneous

105. Cooksey, F. S., *Rehabilitation of the Disabled Housewife.* 12 pp. London: King's College Hospital, 1952.
105a. Cosgrove, Margaret, *A Is for Anatomy.* 63 pp. New York: Dodd, Mead and Company, 1965.
106. Folksam Insurance Company, *Insurance for Handicapped Housewives.* Mimeographed. 7 pp. Stockholm: 1950.
107. Knowles, Esther, and Judson, Julia, *Rehabilitation of Rural Homemakers in Their Own Homes.* 108 pp. Department of Home Economics, University of Vermont, and Office of Vocational Rehabilitation, 1964.
108. Krusen, Frank H., M.D., *Handbook of Physical Medicine and Rehabilitation.* Philadelphia: W. B. Saunders Company, 1965.
109. Switzer, Mary, and Leopold, Alice, *Help for Handicapped Women.* Women's Bureau Pamphlet 5. Illustrated. Bibliography. 52 pp. Washington, D.C.: U.S. Department of Labor, 1958.

Travel

A few references on transportation and accessibility of public places for travelers with physical limitations are listed. Consult the State Department of Motor Vehicles or the Vocational Rehabilitation Administration at the State Capitol of your state, or the Mayor's Office in the city of special interest for specific information.

110. Farkus, J. G., *Where Turning Wheels Stop.* Swissville: Paralyzed Veterans of America, 1960.
111. *The Physically Disabled and Their Environment.* 208 pp. New York: International Society of the Rehabilitation of the Disabled, 1961.
112. Schnur, Sandra, *New York with Ease.* 64 pp. Association for Crippled Children and Adults of New York State, Incorporated.
113. We, the Handicapped, Inc., *Automobile Driving Controls for the Physically Disabled.* Illustrated. Planographed. Spiral binding. Detroit: 1954 (H).
114. ——— *Travel Aids for the Invalid and Disabled.* Illustrated. Planographed. Spiral binding. Detroit: 1954.

Visual Aids for Teaching Homemaking to the Handicapped

Motion Pictures

Produced by School of Home Economics, Audio Visual Center, University of Connecticut. Rental fee, $1.00.

115. *An Approach to Work Simplification for Handicapped Homemakers.* 16 mm., sound, color, 18 mins., 1960. This film presents an organized procedure for finding ways to simplify homemaking tasks.
116. *Principles of Motion Economy Illustrated by Handicapped Homemakers.* 16 mm., sound, color, 18 mins., 1960. In this film, physically handicapped women illustrate the sixteen principles of motion economy most commonly used in homemaking tasks.

117. *Work Simplification Demonstrated by a One-Handed Mother in Bathing a Baby.* 16 mm., sound, color, 12 mins., 1960. The application of fourteen principles of work simplification to a specific job and a specific disability.
118. *Work Simplification Demonstrated by a Wheelchair Mother in Preparing a Formula.* 16 mm., sound, color, 12 mins., 1960. The application of fifteen principles of work simplification to a specific job and a specific disability.
119. *The Best Things in Life.* 16 mm., sound, color, 25 mins., 1960. The film tells a convincing story of how five physically handicapped women share play activities with their young children. It includes crafts, music, nature study, and suggestions for backyard playgrounds and equipment for active indoor play.
120. *Child Care Problems of Physically Handicapped Mothers.* 16 mm., sound, color, 30 mins., 1957. A film designed primarily to orient professional and lay audiences to the problems which orthopedically handicapped homemakers face in caring for young children. (Cleared for general use and closed circuit television only.)
121. *Where There's a Will.* 16 mm., sound, color, 28 mins., 1957. This film includes an introduction by Dr. Lilliam M. Gilbreth and portrays various ways in which four handicapped mothers have made remarkable adjustments in order to resume their homemaking and child care responsibilities.

Visual Auditory Production Center, Wayne University
122. *Take It Easy.* 16 mm., sound, color, 21 mins. A cardiac housewife demonstrates to all homemakers ways to make housekeeping tasks simpler. (Available from regional offices of the American Heart Association.)

International Society for the Rehabilitation of the Disabled.
123. *Handicapped Housewife.* 16 mm., sound, B/W, 16 mins. This film shows a Swedish housewife, limited to the use of one arm, who demonstrates the way in which she bathes her baby.

Audio Visual Center, University of Illinois
124. *Wheelchair Kitchen.* 16 mm., sound, B/W, 4½ mins. A very brief film showsome of the research methods used in developing the bulletin on "Kitchens for Women in Wheelchairs" (A-81).

American Medical Association Film Library
125. *Rehabilitation Adds Years to Life.* 16mm., sound, color, 30 mins. Includes cardiac housewife with other types of disability. Demonstrates community services in action and the role of the doctor on the rehabilitation team.

Association for Aid of Crippled Children, Division of Publications
126. *Dynamic Posture.* 16 mm., sound, color (4 rolls), 24 mins. each. A teaching film dealing with the importance of good posture in lying, sitting, and standing.

Visual Education Branch, Saskatchewan Department of Education
127. *Teaching Cerebral Palsied to Cook.* 16 mm., sound, B/W, 20 mins. A portrayal of the problems of young adults with cerebral palsy in a training class at the rehabilitation center in Regina.

Filmstrips and Slide Series

Consumers Power Company
128. *Easy Does It.* 33 slides of a demonstration kitchen designed to save time and energy.

Photo Lab, Incorporated
129. *Beltsville Energy-Saving Kitchen Workroom.* Filmstrip #c-58. Produced by the United States Department of Agriculture, Agricultural Research Service, Clothing and Research Division. A filmstrip showing the development of energy-saving kitchens.

National Society for Crippled Children and Adults
130. *Architectural Barriers.* A filmstrip designed to make the public aware of the architectural barriers that make it difficult and often impossible for handicapped persons to get into churches, museums, theaters, post offices, stores, and public buildings or to use their facilities.

Handicapped Homemaker Research Center, School of Home Economics, University of Connecticut
131. *A Wheelchair Mother Prepares Baby's Formula.* 19 slides. Shows how a mother confined to a wheelchair applies principles of work simplification to the job of formula preparation. 1960. ($7.00 per set)
132. *Principle of Work Simplification Illustrated by Baby Bathing with Hand Limitations.* 15 slides. Shows how a woman limited to the use of one hand applied the principles of work simplification to the task of bathing and dressing her baby. 1960. ($6.00 per set)
133. *You Can Do Family Laundry with Hand Limitations.* 25 slides. Shows how a woman limited to the use of one hand can do the family laundry. 1960. ($9.00 per set)

Institute of Physical Medicine and Rehabilitation
134. *A Severely Handicapped Homemaker Goes Back to Work in Her Own Kitchen.* Filmstrip. A case study of the adaptation of a kitchen to suit the homemaker's disability.

Plays
135. *Heart of the House,* Nora Stirling. Written for the Vocational Rehabilitation Administration, U.S. Department of Health, Education, and Welfare. Information from *Plays for Living*, Family Service Association of America.

Exhibit of Clothing
136. *Self-Help Clothing for Handicapped Children.* A collection of children's garments selected from the retail market with adaptations to suit disabilities. Eight accompanying charts denote features to look for. National Society for Crippled Children and Adults.

Bibliography Supplement

Barrier Free Design

1. Abeson, Alan, and Blacklow, Julie, *Environmental Design.* Arlington, Va.: The Council for Exceptional Children, 1971, 120 pp.
2. Arneson, Kathaleen C., "Accent on Access." *Rehabilitation Record,* November-December 1966.
3. American Society of Landscape Architects Foundation. *Guidebook on the Design of Outdoor Facilities.* Washington, D.C.: The Foundation, 1973.
4. Bureau of Outdoor Recreation, *Outdoor Recreation Planning For the Handicapped.* Washington, D.C.: The Bureau, 1967.
5. Dreyfuss, Henry, *The Measure of Man: Human Factors in Design,* second ed. New York: Whitney Library of Design, 1967.
6. Finnish Association of Disabled Civilians and Servicemen, *How to Abolish Ambulatory Barriers.* The Association, 1965, 60 pp.
7. Georgia State Department of Parks, *Outdoor Recreation Facilities For the Disabled in Fort Yargo State Park.* Georgia State Park Department.
8. Goldsmith, Selwyn, et-al, "Designing a Public Facility for the Disabled." *Annals of Physical Medicine,* November 1966, 10 pp.
9. Green, Gordon H., *"Removing Barriers From the Pathways of the Handicapped," Human Needs,* February 1973, 4 pp.
10. Gutman, Ernest M., *Wheelchair to Independence: Architectural Barriers Eliminated.* Springfield, Ill.: Charles C. Thomas, 1968, 136 pp.
11. Hilleary, James F., *Buildings For All to Use.* Chicago: National Easter Seal Society, 1969.
12. Klement, Susan, *The Elimination of Architectural Barriers to the Disabled.* Toronto: Canadian Rehabilitation Council, 1969, a bibliography, 36 pp.
13. Lander, Ruth, *The Goal Is—Mobility.* Washington, D.C.: Superintendent of Documents, 1970, 72 pp.
14. McGowan, John F., and Gust, Tim, *Preparing Higher Education Facilities for Handicapped Students.* Columbia: University of Missouri, Services for the Handicapped, 1968, 102 pp.
15. National Commission on Architectural Barriers to Rehabilitation of the Handicapped, *Designs For All Americans,* Washington, D.C.: Superintendent of Documents, 1967.

16. National Easter Seal Society for Crippled Children and Adults. *Current Materials Available on Architectural Barriers.* Chicago: The Society, 1973.
17. National League of Cities, *State and Local Efforts to Remove Architectural Barriers to the Handicapped.* Washington, D.C.: The League, 1967, 162 pp.
18. New York State Council of Parks and Outdoor Recreation, *Outdoor Recreation For the Physically Handicapped. A Handbook of Design Standards.* Albany, New York, 1967.
19. New York State University Construction Fund, *Making Facilities Available to the Physically Handicapped.* Albany, New York: The Fund, 1967, 40 pp.
20. Nugent, Timothy J., "The Challenge of the Disabled and the Aging; New Avenues of Life." *Rehabilitation,* April-June, 1966, 10 pp.
21. Nygren, Alf, *Sports and Open Air Facilities For the Handicapped.* Bromma, Sweden: I.C.T.A. Information Center.
22. President's Committee on Employment of the Handicapped, *News Letter, Committee on Barrier Free Design.* Washington, D.C.: The Committee, 1973.
23. Rehabilitation International U.S.A., *Brochure on Symbol of Access.* New York: Rehabilitation International U.S.A., 1972.
24. State Department of Forests, *Information on Recreational Areas Accessible to the Handicapped.* (Send inquiry to your State Office.)
25. State Department of Parks, *Information on Parks and Recreation Areas Accessible to the Handicapped.* (Send inquiry to your State Office.)
26. Thayer, Robert L., Jr., *Trails For All the People.* Denver, Colo.: Division of Game, Fish and Parks.
27. U.S.D.A. Forest Service, *The Development of Trout Pond Park for the Handicapped.* Tallahassee: Forest Supervisor.
28. Westchester County Easter Seal Society, *Construction Details—Planning For the Handicapped.* The Society, 1971.
29. Yuker, Harold C., *The Development of An Inexpensive Elevator for Eliminating Architectural Barriers.* New York: Hofstra University, 1966, 61 pp.

Children and Youth

1. Barnett, Marian Willer, *Handicapped Girls—Girl Scouting, A Guide for Leaders.* New York Girl Scouts of the U.S.A., 1968.
2. Boy Scouts of America, *Scouting for the Physically Handicapped,* 1971.
   _____, *Scouting For the Visually Handicapped.* 1968.
   _____, *Scouting For the Mentally Retarded.* New Brunswick, Boy Scouts, 1967.
3. Camp Fire Girls, *Leaders of Handicapped Girls.* New York: Camp Fire Girls, Inc., 16 pp.
4. I.C.T.A. Information Center, *Technical Aids for Physically Handicapped Children.* Bromma, Sweden, 1972, 87 pp.
5. Logan, J. A., *There is More to Toys than Meets the Eye.* Chicago: National Easter Seal Society, 1957, 6 pp.

6. Maternal and Child Health Services, *Publications For Parents*. Rockville, Maryland: M.C.H. Service, 1971.
7. National Easter Seal Society, *On Being the Parent of a Handicapped Child* and *You Are Not Alone*. Two of the Parent Series Publications. Chicago: The Society.
8. National Foundation–March of Dimes, *Operation Birthright*. White Plains: National Foundation, 1971, 14 pp.

Clothing

1. Barton, Dorothea, H., *Self-Help Clothing*. Harvest Years, March 1973, pp. 19–23.
2. Bohnekamp, E., "Clothing for the Handicapped." *Orthopedic and Prosthetic Appliance Journal*, March 1967, pp. 61–65.
3. Disabled Living Foundation, *Clothing Fastenings for the Handicapped and Disabled*. London: The Foundation, 1968, 48 pp.
4. _____, *Clothing and the Incontinent Older Child*. March 1972, 3 pp.
5. _____, *Clothing for Wheelchair Users*. September 1971, 5 pp.
6. Friend, Shirley E., Zaccagnini, Judith, Sullivan, Marilyn G., "Meeting Clothing Needs of Handicapped Children." Washington: *Journal of Home Economics*, May 1973.
7. Gamwell, Ann M. and Joyce, Florence. *Problems of Clothing for the Sick and Disabled*. London: Central Council for the Disabled, 1966, 72 pp.
8. Hallenbeck, Phyllis N., "Special Clothing for the Handicapped: Review of Research and Resources." *Rehabilitation Literature*, February, 1966, pp. 34–40.
9. I.C.T.A. Information Center, *Clothing—Suggestions for the Physically Handicapped*. Bromma, Sweden: December, 1971, 19 pp.
10. Lord, Joan, *Catalogue of Garments for the Handicapped and Disabled*. King Edward's Hospital Fund for London for the Shirley Institute, Manchester, England: 1972, vols. 1 and 2.
11. Macnaughtan, Aline K. M., *Clothing for the Limb Deficient Child*. Scottish Branch of the Society for the Aid of Thalidomide Children, Ltd., 1968, 30 pp.
12. National Seminar Report, Social and Rehabilitation Service, H.E.W., *Functionally Designed Clothing and Aids for Chronically Ill and Disabled*. Cleveland, Ohio: Vocational Guidance and Rehabilitation Services, 1966, 18 pp.
13. Newton, Audrey, "Clothing: A Rehabilitation Tool for the Handicapped." *Journal of Home Economics*, April 1973, 2 pp.
14. Schwab, Lois O. and Sindelar, Margaret B., "Clothing for the Physically Disabled Homemaker." *Rehabilitation Record*, March-April 1973, pp. 30–34.
15. Swedish Institute For the Handicapped, *Clothing Suggestions For the Physically Handicapped*. Bromma, Sweden: I.C.T.A. Information Center, 1971, 19 pp.
16. Tudor, Marion, *Senior Citizen, Look Your Best*. Extension Service, North Dakota State University.

17. U.S. Public Health Service, *Flexible Fashions: Clothing Tips and Ideas for the Woman with Arthritis.* Washington, D.C.: Public Health Service Pub. No. 1814, 1968, 28 pp.

Devices—Books, Pamphlets, Bibliographies

1. American Foundation for the Blind, *Aids and Appliances.* 18th edition. New York: The Foundation, 1973.
2. Arkansas Rehabilitation and Training Center, *Assistive Devices and Equipment for Rehabilitation.* Hot Springs, Arkansas: The Center.
3. Fashion-Able, *Self Help Devices for Independent Living.* Rocky Hill, New Jersey, 1973, 24 pp.
4. I.C.T.A. Information Center, Set of Loose-Leaf Sheets on Technical Aids in four languages. Bromma, Sweden: The Center.
5. Institute of Rehabilitation Medicine, *Bibliography on Self Help Devices and Orthotics, 1950–1967.* New York City: The Institute, 1968, 61 pp.
6. Lowman, Edward W., and Klinger, Judith, *Aids to Independent Living: Self Help For the Handicapped.* New York: McGraw-Hill, 1970, 832 pp., 2,237 illustrations.
7. National Easter Seal Society for Crippled Children and Adults, *Reference List on Self Help Devices for the Handicapped.* Chicago: The Society, 1972.
8. Rosenberg, Charlot, *Assistive Devices For the Handicapped.* Minneapolis: American Rehabilitation Foundation, 1968.
9. Zimmerman, Muriel, *Self Help Devices For Rehabilitation,* Part I, 1958 and Part II, 1965. Dubuque, Iowa: William C. Brown Co.

Education

1. Bookmobile and Home Library Service (call your local library or write American Library Association for information).
2. Council of Better Business Bureaus, *Tips on Home Study Schools.* Washington, D.C.: The Bureau, 1972.
3. Dale, Brian, *Canadian Public Libraries and the Physically Handicapped* Toronto: Canadian Rehabilitation Council for the Disabled, 1972.
4. Home Study Courses (write your local superintendent of schools and the universities in your state).
5. President's Committee On Employment of the Handicapped (Education Committee), *Accessibility of Junior Colleges for Handicapped,* Washington, D.C.: U.S. Government Printing Office, 1972.
6. National Home Study Council, *Directory of Accredited Private Home Study Schools.* The Council, 1973.
7. National Paraplegia Foundation, *Colleges and Universities with Provisions For Wheelchair Students.* Washington, D.C.: N.P.F.
8. Library of Congress Division of the Blind and Physically Handicapped, *Talking Book Topics,* March-April, 1973. Washington: The Library.

Family Relations

1. Ayrault, Evelyn West, *Helping the Handicapped Teenager to Mature.* New York: Association Press, 1971.
2. Griffith, Ernest R., Timms, Robert J., and Tomko, Michael A., *Sexual Problems of Patients with Spinal Cord Injuries: An Annotated Bibliography.* U. Cincinnati, Medical Center. 1973.
3. Holman, George W., "Considerations in Management of Psychosexual Readjustments in the Cord Injured Male." *Rehabilitation Psychology,* 1972, vol. 19, no. 2, 8 pp. (rewritten for *Paraplegia News,* February, 1973, and titled, "Sex and The Spinal Cord Injured Male").
4. Lancaster, Gaye Derek (ed.) *Personal Relationships, the Handicapped and the Community.* (Programs in Holland, Sweden, England and Denmark). New York: United Cerebral Palsy Society, 1972, 150 pp.
5. McKain, Walter C., *Retirement Marriage.* Monograph III. Storrs, Conn.: Connecticut Agricultural Experiment Station 06268.
6. Minnesota Council on Family Relations, *Bibliography Family Life: Literature and Films.* Minneapolis: National Council on Family Relations.
7. Nordquist, Inger (ed.), *Life Together: The Situation of the Handicapped.* Report of the Nordic Seminar on Sexual and Allied Problems Among the Orthopedically Handicapped. Swedish Central Committee For Rehabilitation, 1972, 74 pp.
8. Romano, Mary D., and Lassiter, Robert E., "Sexual Counseling With the Spinal Cord Injured." *Physical Medicine and Rehabilitation,* December 1972, 5 pp.
9. Sex Information and Education Council, *Sexual Life in Later Years.* New York: The Council.
10. United Ostomy Association. *Sex, Pregnancy and the Female Ostomate.* Los Angeles: The Association, 1972, 21 pp.
11. Young, B. M., "Sex and the Handicapped Child." *Rehabilitation Digest,* Spring 1972.

Gardening For the Physically Limited

1. Disabled Living Foundation, *The Easy Path To Gardening.* London: The Readers Digest Association, Limited, 1972, 88 pp.
2. Jon Dol and Associates, *Vertical Gardening Equipment.* The Associates, 1973.
3. Heald, C. B., *Your Garden and Your Rheumatism.* Toronto: Canadian Arthritis and Rheumatism Society, 23 pp.
4. Heffley, Paula Diane, *Horticulture: A Therapeutic Tool.* Journal of Rehabilitation, January-February 1973.
5. I.C.T.A. Information Center, *Gardening For the Disabled.* Bromma, Sweden.
6. Library of Congress, Division For the Blind and Physically Handicapped, *Bibliography, Special Format Books on Gardening.* Washington, D.C.: The Library.

7. Paul, Aileen, *Kids Gardening*. Garden City, New York: Doubleday, 1972, 96 pp.
8. Snook, Leslie, *Gardening For the Elderly and Handicapped*. London: Pan Books, L.T.D., 1968. In U.S.—Walter F. Nicke Company, Box 71, Hudson, New York, 12534.

Health and Safety

1. American Cancer Society, *Care of Your Colostomy*. New York: The Society, 1972.
2. _____, *A Manual of Information for Women Who Have Had Breast Surgery*. The Society, 1972.
3. American Diabetes Association, *Facts About Diabetes*. New York: The Association, 1966.
4. American Heart Association, *Do It Yourself Again, Self Help Devices for the Stroke Patient*. New York: The Association, 1969, 47 pp.
5. _____, *Up and Around*. A booklet to aid the stroke patient in activities of daily living. New York: The Association. 48 pp.
6. Bechill, William D., Wolgamot, Irene, *Nutrition for the Elderly*. Washington, D.C.: Superintendent of Documents, 1973.
7. American Optometric Association, *Driving Tips For Senior Citizens*. New York: The Association (free).
8. American Podiatry Association, *Foot Health and Aging*. Washington, D.C.: The Association (free).
9. Arthritis Foundation, *Home Care Program in Arthritis*. New York: The Foundation, 1969, 23 pp.
10. Family Health Magazine, *Where To Find Information, A Directory of Health Organizations*.
11. Food and Drug Administration, *Some Questions and Answers About Dietary Supplements*. Washington, D.C.: The Administration (free).
12. National Nutrition Information Clearing House, *Nutrition Information for the Whole Family*. Berkeley, California, National Society for Nutrition Education, 1973.
13. Frost, Alma, *Handbook for Paraplegics and Quadriplegics*. National Paraplegia Foundation, 1964, 48 pp.
14. Health Education and Welfare, *Strike Back At Stroke*. New York: American Heart Association, 37 pp.
15. Kavanogh, Terence, *Conditioning in the Elderly*. Toronto: Canadian Rehabilitation Council for the Disabled. Reprinted 1970, 2 pp.
16. National Easter Seal Society, *Safety Check List For the Aging and Handicapped; Home Safety Round-Up; Safety Check For Parents*. Chicago: The Society.
17. National Hearing Aid Society, *How to Choose the Right Hearing Aid for You* (free).
18. National Foundation, March of Dimes, *Facts 1973*. White Plains, New York; The Foundation, 1973, 67 pp.
19. National Paraplegia Foundation, *A Basic Library of Paraplegia Publications*. The Foundation, 1973, 7 pp.

20. National Paraplegia Foundation, *How to Get Help if You Are Paralyzed*. 15 pp.
21. National Safety Council, *Accident Facts 1972 Edition*.
22. Nutrition Foundation, *Your Diet: Health is in the Balance*. New York: The Foundation.
23. Office of Consumer Services, *Consumer Information Series* on Nursing Home Care, Tooth Care, Medicine and other health topics. U.S. Government Printing Office, 1973.
24. Public Affairs Pamphlets, *Better Health In Later Years*.
25. ————. When Mental Illness Strikes Your Family. New York: Public Affairs Publications.
26. Sarno, John E. and Sarno, Martha T., *Stroke, The Condition and the Patient*, New York: McGraw-Hill.
27. Schweekert, Harry A., Jr., *Bibliography for Use of Paraplegics and Quadriplegics*, Washington: Paralyzed Veterans of America.
28. Social Security Administration, *A Brief Explanation of Medicare*. (Your local office).
29. Superintendent of Documents, lists of publications on many subjects such as health and medical services, diseases and physical conditions. Government Printing Office, 1972.
30. U.S. Department of Housing and Urban Development, *A Design Guide for Home Safety*. (Stock #2300–0201). Washington, D.C.: U.S. Government Printing Office, 1972.
31. Veterans Administration, *Rehabilitating The Person With Spinal Cord Injuries* (a source book). U.S. Government Printing Office, 1972, 58 pp.

Home Management and Homemaking Miscellaneous

1. Burton, A. M. and Trotter, V. Y., *Homemaking Unlimited Series on All Phases of Homemaking*. Lincoln: University of Nebraska, College of Home Economics.
2. Consumer Product Information Center, *An Index of Selected Federal Publications on how to buy, use and take care of Consumer Products*. Pueblo, Colorado: The Center, 1973.
3. Continuing Education in Home Economics, University of Alabama, *On Your Own News Letters*, vol. I, 1971, vol. II, 1972.
4. Dale, Verna, Uhlinger, Susan J., *Resources in Home Economics for the Blind Homemaker*. Amherst, Massachusetts: Massachusetts Home Economics Association, 1969.
5. Fish, Hariet U., *Take It Easy*. Published by the author, 17050 Northrup Way, Bellevue, Washington 98008, 19 pp.
6. Hodgeman, Karen, Warpelia, Eleanor, and Lundberg, Ann, *Adaptations and Techniques For the Disabled Homemaker*. Minneapolis: Sister Kenny Institute, 1973, 26 pp.
7. Jeffrey, Dorothy A., "A Living Environment for the Physically Disabled." *Rehabilitation Literature*, April 1973, 6 pp. (reprints available).
8. Klinger, Judith L., Friedman, Fred H., and Sullivan, Richard A., *Mealtime Manual For the Aged and the Handicapped*. (Includes manufacturers of assistive devices.) New York: Simon & Schuster 1970.

9. Laging, Barbara, *Furniture Design for the Elderly*. Chicago: National Easter Seal Society, 1966, 10 pp.
10. Library of Congress, Division for the Blind and Physically Handicapped, *Bibliography: Consumer Education and Protection*. Washington, D.C.: The Library.
11. National Council on Aging, *Furniture Requirements For Older People*. The Council, 1963, 46 pp.
12. Schwab, Lois O., "The Home Economist in Rehabilitation." *Rehabilitation Literature*, May 1968, 8 pp.
13. Schwab, Lois, Trotter, Virginia, *Homemaker Rehabilitation: A Selected Bibliography*. Washington, D.C.: Women's Committee, President's Committee on Employment of the Handicapped, 1972.
14. Smith, Frances M., *Supplement Resources in Home Economics for the Blind Homemaker*. Amherst, Massachusetts: Massachusetts Home Economics Association, 1972.
15. U.S. Department of Agriculture, *Popular Publications on Homemaking*. List No. 5, The Department, 1972.

Housing

1. Administration on Aging, *Housing and Living Arrangements for Older People*. Washington, D.C.: The Administration.
2. Balkems, John B., *Housing and Living Arrangements for Older People. A Bibliography. Washington, D.C.:* National Council on Aging, 1972.
3. I.C.T.A. Information Center, *Architectural Facilities for the Disabled*. Bromma, Sweden: The Center, 1973, 32 pp.
4. Langing, Barbara, *How to Design a Non-Person: A Critical Look at the Environment For the Elderly*. New York: National Society of Interior Designers, 1971, 7 pp.
5. McGuire, Marie C., *Design of Housing For the Elderly* (a check list). Washington, D.C.: National Association of Housing and Redevelopment Officials, 1972.
6. Laurie, Gini, *Housing and Home Services For the Disabled in the United States and in Quadalayara, Mexico. Rehabilitation Gazette*, Annual Issue, 1973 (reprint available), 7 pp.
7. Small Homes Council, *Publications*. Urbana, Ill.: University of Illinois 1972.
8. Smith, Carol R., *Home Planning for the Severely Disabled*. Medical Clinics of North America, May 1969. (Available Institute Rehabilitation Medicine.)
9. U.S. Department of Housing and Urban Development, *The Built Environment For the Elderly and The Handicapped: A Bibliography*. Washington, D.C.: Superintendent of Documents #2300–1191, 1971, 46 pp.
10. ———, *Housing For the Physically Impaired*. A guide for planning and design. Superintendent of Documents, 1968.
11. Veterans Administration, *Model Housing Units for Paraplegics* (also useful for information on grants and loans), Washington, D.C.: The Administration.

Motion Pictures, Slides and Filmstrips

Lists available on request. Indicate area of interest. See Appendix G for addresses.

1. Administration on Aging, H.E.W.
2. American Home Economics Association.
3. Cornell University, Film Library.
4. Hofstra University.
5. International Film Bureau.
6. Learning Resource Facility, Institute Physical Medicine
7. Library of Congress.
8. Minnesota Society for Crippled Children and Adults.
9. National Audiovisual Center.
10. National Council on the Aging.
11. National Easter Seal Society For Crippled Children and Adults.
12. National Medical Audiovisual Center.
13. President's Committee on Employment of the Handicapped.
14. Rehabilitation International U.S.A. Film Library.
15. Social and Rehabilitation Services Administration, H.E.W.
16. State University Construction Fund.
17. U.S. Department of Agriculture.
18. University of Connecticut, Audiovisual Department.
19. University of Connecticut, School of Home Economics.
20. University of Nebraska, College of Home Economics.
21. University of Colorado, Audiovisual Service.

Rehabilitation

1. Dean, Russel J. N., *New Life for Millions*. New York: Hastings House, 1972.
2. Human Resources Center, *Human Resources Monographs*. Albertson, L.I.: The Center, 1967.
3. I.C.T.A. Information Service, *List of Literature*. Bromma, Sweden: 1972.
4. Institute of Rehabilitation Medicine, *Rehabilitation Monograph XXXV*. New York: The Institute.
5. National Congress of Organizations of the Physically Handicapped, *Roster of Organizations of the Physically Handicapped and Their Chapters*, third ed. The Congress of Organizations, 1970.
6. National Easter Seal Society, *When You Meet a Handicapped Person*. Chicago: The Society, 4 pp.
7. _____, *A Selected List of Periodicals that Publish Articles Concerning the Handicapped*. The Society, 1972, 11 pp.
8. National Institute of Neurological Diseases, *Spinal Cord Injury*. Public Health Service Bulletin #1747, Washington, D.C.: U.S. Government Printing Office, 1969.
9. National Paraplegia Foundation, *Basic Library of Paraplegia Publications, Annotated bibliography*. Chicago: The Foundation, 7 pp.

10. National Rehabilitation Association, *Journal of Rehabilitation.* Washington, D.C.: The Association (monthly)
11. Rehabilitation International, List of *Publications and Films,* New York: Information Secretary, Rehabilitation International.
12. Safilios, Rothchild, C., "Social Integration of the Disabled," *Rehabilitation Digest,* Fall 1972.
13. President's Committee on Employment of the Handicapped, Women's Committee, Bibiography, Homemaker Rehabilitation. The Committee, 1972.
14. Rehabilitation Services Administration (H.E.W.) *For the Disabled—Help Through Rehabilitation.* S.R.S. 1972.
15. Rehabilitation Services Administration, *Mobility For Handicapped Students.* Washington, D.C.: H.E.W.
16. Rusk, Howard A. et al., *Rehabilitation Medicine* third ed., St. Louis, Missouri:
17. Rusk, Howard A., *A World To Care For.* New York: Random House, 1973.
18. Wright, Beatrice A., *Disabling Myths About Disability.* Chicago: National Easter Seal Society, 1961, 11 pp.
19. Works, Nora, *You on Crutches, How to Help Them Help You.* New York, Carlton Press, 1968.

"65 Plus"

1. Administration on Aging, *More Words on Aging.* Bibliography Supplement, The Administration, 1971.
2. American Association of Retired Persons and National Retired Teachers Association, *Better Retirement Guide Series* (includes ten different publications). 1972.
3. American Dietetic Association, *Forget Birthdays, Enjoy Good Eating.* Bibliography, The Association.
4. American Home Economics Association, "Working with the Elderly," *Journal of Home Economics,* April 1973.
5. Atchley, R., *The Social Forces in Later Life.* Belmont, California: Wadworth, 1972.
6. Bell, William G., *Community Care for the Elderly An Alternative to Institutionalization.* Tallahassee: Florida State University.
7. Busse, E., Pfeiffer, E., *Behavior and Adaptation to Later Life.* Boston: Little, Brown, 1969.
8. Degen, Charles, *Age Without Fear.* Jerico, New York: Exposition Press, 1972, 144 pp.
9. Dugan, Maida M., "I'm Staying At Home" and Shellahy, Robert K., "But If You Have to Sell." *Modern Maturity,* June-July 1973.
10. Fish, Harriet U., *Activities Program for Senior Citizens.* West Nyack, New York: Parker Publishing Co., 1971.
11. Fritz, Dorothy B., *Growing Old is a Family Affair.* Richmond: John Knox Press, 1972.
12. Hoffman, Adeline M., ed., *The Daily Needs and Interests of Older People,* Springfield, Ill.: Charles C. Thomas, 1970, 493 pp.

13. Institute of Lifetime Learning, *Lifetime Learning*. Washington, D.C.: The Institute (free).
14. Meeks, Carol, *Where to Find It. Useful Information for Older People*. Amherst, Massachusetts: Cooperative Extension Service, 1973, 15 pp.
15. Merrill, Toni, *Social Clubs for the Aging*. Springfield, Ill.: Charles C. Thomas, 1973.
16. Michigan-Wayne State Institute of Gerontology, *Bibliographies in Twenty Areas of Education*. Ann Arbor: University of Michigan Press, 1972.
17. National Council on Aging, List of *Annotated Bibliographies*. Washington, D.C.: The Council, 1972.
18. National Senior Citizens Law Center, *The Advocates Handbook*, The Center, 1972, 67 pp.
19. Palmore, Erdman, "The Puzzle of Aging." *Family Health*, March 1973.
20. Pollard, Lulu, *Retirement, Black and White*. New York: Exposition Press, 1973.
21. Smith, Elliott D., *Handbook of Aging: For Those Growing Old and Those Concerned with Them*. New York: Harper & Row, 1973.
22. Superintendent of Documents, *Social Services, Aging, Retirement and Social Welfare*. Price List 78, Government Printing Office, May 1973.
23. _____, *Transition, A Guide to Retirement*. Washington, D.C.: U.S. Government Printing Office, 1973.
24. VanDyke, Frank, and Brown, Virginia, *Organized Home Care: An Alternative to Institutions*.
25. White House Conference on Aging, *Toward A National Policy on Aging*. vols. I and II, Final Report 1971., Superintendent of Documents.
26. White House Conference on Aging, *Recommendations for Action* (covers twenty-three areas). 1971, Superintendent of Documents.

Sports, Trails, Camping, Recreation Miscellaneous

1. American Association for Health, Physical Education and Recreation, *Information Service, Programs for the Handicapped*. Washington, D.C.: A.A.H.P., 1973.
2. American National Red Cross, *Swimming For the Handicapped*. Washington, D.C.: A.N.R.C.
3. Avedon, Elliott M., "Outdoor Facilities for the Aged and Disabled." *Parks and Recreation*, May 1966, 4 pp.
4. Buell, Charles, *Recreation for the Blind*. New York: American Foundation for the Blind.
5. Bureau of Outdoor Recreation, *Outdoor Recreation Space Standards*.
6. _____, *Outdoor Recreation Planning for the Handicapped*. U.S. Department of the Interior, 1967.
7. Canadian Stage and Arts Publications, *Riding for Rehabilitation. A Guide for Handicapped Riders and Their Instructors*. C.S.A.P., 49 Wellington Street, East, Toronto, Ontario, Canada.
8. Carroll, Arthur J., "Efforts to Adapt National Forest Recreation Areas for Use by the Handicapped." *Therapeutic Recreation Journal*, First Quarter, 1973.

9. Center for Leisure Studies, *Training Needs and Strategies in Camping for the Handicapped*. Eugene, Oregon: The Center, 1973.

10. Council for National Cooperation in Aquatics and American Association for Health, Physical Education and Recreation, *Aquatics For the Impaired, Disabled, and Handicapped*. American Association H.P.E.R.

11. Disabled Living Foundation, *Sport and Physical Recreation for the Disabled*. 23 pp. *Music and the Physically Handicapped*. 24 pp., The Foundation.

12. Droege, Richard F., *"Giving Handicaps the Heave-ho: Braille Trails and Lion's Tales."* Washington, D.C.: *The Yearbook of Agriculture, 1972,* 4 pp.

13. Inyo National Forest Staff, *Planning Outdoor Recreation Facilities for the Handicapped*. U.S. Forest Service, 1971, 24 pp.

14. Merrill, Toni, *Activities For the Aged and Infirm*. Springfield, Ill.: Charles C. Thomas, 1967.

15. National Easter Seal Society For Crippled Children and Adults, *Directory of Resident Camps for People With Special Health Needs*. Chicago: The Society, 1973.

16. National Park Service, *National Park Guide For the Handicapped*. Superintendent of Documents, 1971.

17. National Parks and Recreation Association, *Literature Kit: Recreation for the Handicapped*. The Association.

18. National Therapeutic Recreation Society, *Publications on Indoor and Outdoor Recreation for the Handicapped*. Arlington, Virginia: The Society, 1973.

19. Nesbitt, John A., (ed.), Brown, Paul D. and Murphy, James F., *Recreation and Leisure Services for the Disadvantaged*. Philadelphia: Lea and Febiger, 1970, 593 pp.

20. Nesbitt, John A., Hansen, Curtis C., Bates, Barbara J. and Neal, Larry L., *Training Needs and Strategies in Camping for the Handicapped*. Eugene, Oregon: Center of Leisure Studies, 1972.

21. Nygren, Alf.; Perryd, Stig; Söderström, Sten, *Sports and Open Air Facilities*. I.C.T.A.

22. President's Committee on Employment of the Handicapped, *Guide to the National Parks and Monuments for the Handicapped Tourist*. Washington, D.C.: The Committee.

23. _____, *News Letter, The Committee on Recreation and Leisure*. Washington, D.C.: The Committee.

24. Recreation Center For the Handicapped, *List of Publications*. San Francisco: The Center, 1973.

25. San Bernardino National Forest, *Interpretive Trails for the Handicapped*. Whispering Pine Nature Trail, U.S. Forest Service, 1969.

26. Schuster, Steve "If I Can Do This—I Can Do Anything." *Snow Sports,* December 1969.

27. State of Georgia Parks Department, *Outdoor Recreation Facilities for the Handicapped*. Fort Yargo State Park: Atlanta: The Department, 1971, 27 pp.

28. Stevens, Ardis, *Fun is Therapeutic* (a book for therapeutic recreation leaders). Springfield, Ill.: Charles C. Thomas, 1971.

250

29. Stone, Edward H., *There's A Wheelchair in the Woods*. U.S. Forest Service, Information Office.
30. Thayer, Robert L., Jr., *Trails For All the People*. Denver: Colorado Division of Game Fish and Parks, 1972.
31. U.S. Forest Service, *Information on Trails and Camps for the Handicapped in National Forests*. Washington, D.C.: U.S. Forest Service, Information Office.
32. Van Orden, H. E., "Family Camping for the Handicapped." Washington, D.C.: *Rehabilitation Record*, May-June 1973.
33. Witt, Peter A. and Wilt, Jo E., "Recreation for Special Groups." *Rehabilitation Digest*, Summer 1972.

Transportation and Travel

1. Accent on Living Magazine, *Survey of Special Laws for Handicapped Drivers*. The Magazine, Fall, 1973.
2. American Automobile Association, *Vehicle Controls for Disabled Persons* (free). Washington, D.C.: A.A.A., 1973, 4 pp.
3. Annand Douglas, *The Wheelchair Traveler*. Published by the author, Ball Hill Road, Milford, New Hampshire 03055, 1973.
4. Bean, William, "Transportation Overview." *Rehabilitation Record* (includes five articles on the subject of transportation), July-August 1972.
5. Bray and Cunningham, *"Vehicles For the Severely Disabled"* (reprint). Chicago: *Rehabilitation Literature*, April 1967.
6. Everest and Jennings, *Many Roads, A Guide for Wheelchair Users*. Published by the authors, Los Angeles, 1972.
7. Gutman, Ernest, *Travel Guide for the Disabled*. Springfield, Ill.: Charles C. Thomas.
8. Hogsett, Stanley G., *Airline Transportation for the Handicapped and Disabled*. Chicago: National Easter Seal Society, 1972.
9. Mobile Homes Manufacturing Association, *Consumer Facts About Mobile Home Living*. Bibliography, The Association 1973.
10. President's Committee on Employment of the Handicapped (Women's Committee), *A List of Guidebooks for Handicapped Travelers*. Washington, D.C.: The Committee, 1972.
11. _____, *Highway Rest Area Facilities–Designed For Handicapped Travelers*. Washington, D.C.: The Committee, 1972.
12. _____, *Airport Terminals and the Physically Handicapped*. Washington: The Committee, 1973.
13. Rehabilitation Gazette, *Vans, Buses, Hydraulic Lifts, and Public Transportation*. St. Louis, Missouri: The Gazette, 1973.
14. Rehabilitation International. *Foreign Travel Guides For the Handicapped*. New York: R.I., 1973.
15. Rehabilitation Record, *Transportation and Travel Issue*. July-August 1972.
16. Urban Mass Transportation Administration, Report on *Conference on Transportation and Human Needs*. Washington, D.C.: The Administration, 1972.

17. _____, *Provisions for the Elderly and Handicapped in the Design of Transbus*, 1973.
18. Villarreal, Carlos C., "Helping the Aged Get Around." *Human Needs*, January 1973.

A Few of the Travel Service Agencies with Tours Arranged For the Handicapped and the Elderly

1. American Association of Retired Persons
2. Bridge Travel Service
3. Evergreen Travel Service
4. Judd's Travel Headquarters
5. National Retired Teachers Association
6. See Airlines for Special Tours

Volunteer Work and Employment

1. Administration on Aging, *Fact Sheet on Employment and Volunteer Opportunities For Older People* (free). Includes such projects as: Foster Grandparents Program, Peace Corps, Vista, Senior Aids, SCORE, ACE. See Appendix G.
2. Employment Services: State and Municipal Departments of Labor, Local and State Veterans Employment Services.
3. Health, Education and Welfare, *Manual on Volunteer Services in Public Welfare and Social Services*. Superintendent of Documents, 1972.
4. International Association of Rehabilitation Facilities, *Volunteers For People in Need*. A Conference Report, 1972, 159 pp.
5. Manpower Administration, *Older Workers, Manpower Programs for Senior Citizens* (free), 1973.
6. President's Committee on Employment of the Handicapped, *Employment Assistance for the Handicapped*, Directory of Federal and State Programs. The Committee, 1973, 37 pp. In your own state write Governor's Committee on Employment of the Handicapped.
7. State Commission on Aging. Write your state office for opportunities for volunteer work and paid employment.
8. Veterans Hospitals. Contact the Director of Voluntary Services in your nearest hospital.

Credits for
Photographs
and Drawings

Photographs are listed below by country of origin. All photographs not listed below were made by Jerauld A. Manter, Storrs, Connecticut. All pen and ink drawings except for those indicated below were made by Professor Eleanor Boettke Hotte, Department of Clothing, Textiles and Related Art, School of Home Economics, University of Connecticut, Storrs, Connecticut.

Australia
1. Australian Red Cross, N.S.W. Division: p. 126, center.

Bangladesh
2. Hug, Mrs. Mohammad Shamsul, Dacca: p. 170 center left and right.

Canada
3. Public Health Restoration Center, courtesy Saskatchewan Government Photographic Services: p. 4, top; p. 6, bottom; p. 124, bottom; p. 131, top left; p. 132, bottom; p. 145, top.

Denmark
4. Orthopedic Hospital, Copenhagen: p. 11, bottom; p. 125; p. 135, bottom left; p. 139, top left.
5. Testing and Observation Institute of the Danish National Association for Infantile Paralysis: p. 162.

Finland

6. Home for the Aged, Helsinki: p. 193, upper right; p. 196.
7. Invalid Foundation Orthopedic Hospital, Helsinski: p. 126, top left; p. 127, top; p. 127, bottom right; p. 133, center, Valok E. Tolvanen, photographer.
8. Kivela Hospital, Helsinki, Valok E. Tolvanen, photographer: p. 140, top.
9. School and Foundation for Cripples, Helsinki, Valok E. Tolvanen, photographer: p. 10, top; p. 11, center; p. 28, top; p. 127, bottom left.

France

10. Raymond Poincare Hospital, Garches: p. 128, bottom right; p. 131, bottom right; p. 166.
11. Mme. M. L. Lemonnier, Paris: p. xii (opposite p. 1), bottom two.

Great Britain

12. Central Council for the Aid of Cripples, London, Hampshire Co. Council: p. 168; C. Wycliffe Noble F.R.I.B.A. Research Architect; p. 139, bottom right.
13. Disabled Living Foundation, London: p. 193, lower left.
14. Princess Margaret Rose Hospital, Edinburgh: p. 12–13.
15. Scottish Council for the Care of Spastics, Edinburgh: p. 145, bottom right.
16. The Women's Voluntary Service Housing Association and John Laing and Son, Ltd.: p. 169; p. xii (opposite p. 1), top.

India

17. All India Institute of Medical Sciences, Department of Social Work, New Delhi: p. 170, top left.
18. Tyagi, S.L., United States Education Foundation in India, New Delhi: p. 152.
19. Y.W.C.A., Madras: p. 170, top right.

The Netherlands

20. Municipal Medical Health Services, Utrecht: p. 167, center and bottom right.
21. Netherlands Central Committee for the Care of Cripples, The Hague: p. 24, bottom; p. 145, center left; p. 154; p. 167, top.

256

Sweden

22. National Swedish Institute for Consumer Information, Stockholm: p. 164, upper left.
23. Swedish Central Committee for the Welfare of Cripples (S.V.C.K.), Bromma: p. 128, top right; p. 136; p. 138, top; p. 144; p. 151, bottom; p. 163; p. 165, top.
24. Olle Blomgrist Co.: p. 165, bottom.

United States

25. Accent on Living: p. 184; p. 185; p. 186.
26. ACTION, "R.S.V.P.:" p. 188; p. 193, lower right; p. 194; p. 195.
27. Bethshears, Mary, photographer, courtesy Fairfield Press, Westport, Conn.: p. 178.
28. Brooks, Marie, Oklahoma City: p. 149, top left; p. 151, top.
29. California Department of Parks and Recreation, Recreation Trails Committee: p. 192, lower right.
30. Cibola National Forest: p. 180.
31. Colorado State University, Occupational Therapy Dept.: p. 5.
32. di Pietro, Joseph, photographer for the Ladies' Home Journal: p. 64, bottom.
33. Erskine, Mrs. Halley, New York: p. 18.
34. "Fashion-Able": p. 95.
35. Four-H Club Girls' Council, Dade County, Florida: p. 103, center.
36. Hamilton, Ann, photographer, Minneapolis: p. 48.
37. Heart Association of Maryland, Baltimore: p. 27, bottom left.
38. Institute of Rehabilitation Medicine, New York University Medical Center: p. 15; p. 16; p. 92; p. 100; p. 101; p. 155; p. 172.
39. Kenny Rehabilitation Institute, Minneapolis: p. 137, lower left.
40. Klaus, Mrs. Caesar, Eureka, Ill.: p. 176; p. 177; p. 209; p. 210.
41. Kossuth, George, photographer, Wheeling, W. Va.: p. 73; p. 75, top right.
42. Letters, R. B., Storrs, Conn.: p. 176; p. 177; p. 209; p. 210.
43. Lewellen, Mrs. Max, Caldwell, Iowa: p. 141, top right.
44. Michigan Heart Association and Home Economics Extension Service, Michigan State University: p. 171.
45. National Safety Council, Chicago: p. 164, top right; p. 164, center left; p. 164, lower right.
46. National Easter Seal Society for Crippled Children and Adults: p. 105.

47. Ohio Goodwill Industries Rehabilitation Center, Cincinnati: p. 142; p. 149, top right; p. 173.
48. Orange County General Hospital, Orange, Calif.: p. 7; p. 27, top; p. 131, bottom left.
49. Pattison, Mrs. Lee, Claremont, California: p. 148, top right and left.
50. Pennsylvania State University, College of Human Development: p. 139, bottom left.
51. President's Committee on Employment of the Handicapped: p. 179; p. 191; p. 192.
52. Rehabilitation Institute of Greater Detroit: p. 137, center right.
53. Rehabilitation Institute of Chicago, Occupational Therapy Dept.: p. 10, bottom; p. 131, upper right.
54. Rubbermaid, Wooster, Ohio: p. 141, center right.
55. School and Hospital for Crippled Children, Sioux Falls, South Dakota: p. 11, top right.
56. Schuster, Steve: p. 182.
57. Ski Touring Council, Troy, Vermont: p. 181.
58. Smith, Cedric H., photographer, Frederick, Md. *News Post:* p. 192, top left.
59. Tuberculosis and Health Association, Bergen County, N.J.: p. 176.
60. United Cerebral Palsy Association of Los Angeles County, Calif.: p. 130, bottom right and left.
61. University of Illinois, Department of Home Economics: p. 160; p. 161.
62. University of Illinois Medical Center, Occupational Therapy Dept.: p. 26, top center.
63. University of Michigan Medical Center, Occupational Therapy Dept.: p. 3; p. 24, top.
64. United States Department of Agriculture, Clothing and Housing Research Division: p. 93; p. 94; p. 174.
65. Veterans' Administration Hospital, East Orange, N.J.: p. 6, top; p. 187.
66. Vocational Guidance and Rehabilitation Service, Cleveland, Ohio; p. 96; p. 97.
67. Walker, Mrs. Margaret Hovey, Pacific Palisades, Calif.: p. 148, bottom left.
68. Walter Reed Army Medical Center, Department of Occupational Therapy: p. 14.
69. Woolverton, Mary, photographer, Fitzsimmons General Hospital, Denver, Colo.: p. 183.

Index

Babies. *See* Infants

Baking. *See* Food Preparation

Balance problems, 25, 41, 44, 158, 159, 193

Bangladesh, research in cooking arrangements, 170. *See also* Credits

Barrier-free design. *See* Architectural Barriers

Bathinettes. *See* Infants and Work Centers

Bathing of infants. *See* Infants, care of

Bathrooms: 48, 138, 158, 165, 167, 169; adjustments in height of equipment, 165, 167, 169; assistive devices for, 165, 167, 169; detachable shower nozzle, 165; heaters for, 169; transfer from wheelchair to tub, 158, 165, 169; Swedish folding tub, 165; wall-hung fixtures, 165, 169

Bechtol, Charles O., ix

Behrens, Dorothy A., 96

Bethshears, Mary, 178. *See also* Credits

Bibliography: 230–252

Bibs, 53

Birth defects, 10, 12, 13

Blind: "braille trails," 180; "talking books," 194; resources for, Appendix G, H, I. *See also* Work simplification

Blouses: girls', 111, 112; slip combinations, 122; women's, 93, 96. *See also* Clothing, selection and adaptation

Body, efficient use of, 26–28

Bookmobiles, 194

Books, for children, 73

Boots and booties, 118, 119. *See also* Infants, clothing for

Bottles and nipples, 49

Bowling, 190, 192

Braces, 84, 98, 100, 109, 113–115, 120

Bras, 95, 99

Brooks, Marie, 149, 151. *See* Credits

Buntings, 53; *See also* Infants, clothing for

Buttons, 79, 101, 113

California Department of Parks and Recreation, Recreation Trails Committee, 192. *See also* Credits

Camping. *See* Recreation

Can and bottle openers, 134, 141

Canada: Canadian Arthritis and Rheumatism Society, *See* Bibliography; Canadian Rehabilitation Council for the Disabled, *See* Bibliography; Public Health Restoration Center, Saskatchewan, 4, 6, 124, 131, 132, 145; *See also* Credits; Rehabilitation Digest; *See* Bibliography

Cars, special equipment for, 184, 176. *See also* Automobiles

Carts: for dressing infants, 25, 204; for bathing infants, 45, 46, 201; for kitchen use, 144, 145; for laundry, 21, 30

Casters, to avoid lifting: 25, 26, 27, 41, 45, 46. *See also* Work Simplification

Census, U.S. *See* Population

Central Council for the Care of Cripples, Great Britain: 139, 168; *See also* Credits and Bibliography

Chairs, for adults, 26; for children, 38, 49, 204; foot-powered, 149; safety precautions for using, 50; safety slip covers, 50, 206; selection of, 39; toilet, 50. *See also* Wheelchairs

Childbearing, 37

Children: care of, 54–77; clothing for, 103–122; growth features of, 110; and independence in dressing, 78–89, 103; of school age, 111–122; self help features for, 78–80, 103–109; creative experiences for, 54–57, 62–72; developing early independence in, 54–62; developing cooperative behavior in, 54–57, 59, 61, 63, 64, 68–77; and handicaps, 9–13, 103–122; and play, 2, 10–13, 53, 55, 62, 63, 64, 68, 70, 72, 74, 77, 150, 180, 194, 195; homemade play equipment for, 56–58, 62, 63; and importance of play, 54, 55, 63–77; and indoor play, 54, 55, 59, 77; and outdoor play, 2, 56–58; safety: 50, 206; play yards, 56; safe toys, 60, 62; safety gates, 61; storage of medicines and cleaning supplies, 164. *See also,* Infants, care of; Clothing, selection and adaptation; and Play

Chronic illnesses, 17, 186, 187. *See* Bibliography

Churches, 175, 176, 188

Cibola National Forest, 180; *See also* Credits

Great Britain: Central Council for the
Care of Cripples, London, 168, 169;
Disabled Living Foundation, 193,
see also Bibliography; Hampshire
County Council and John Lang and
Son, Limited, xii, 169; King's College Hospital, London, 168, *see also*
Bibliography; National Fund for Research into Poliomyelitis and other
Crippling Diseases, *see* Bibliography; C. Wycliffe Noble, F.R.I.B.A.,
139, *see also* Credits; Princess Margaret Rose Hospital, Edinburgh, 12,
13; *Rehabilitation* Magazine, *see*
Appendix H; Royal Devonshire Hospital, 168; Royal Institute of British
Architects, *see* Bibliography; Scottish Council for the Care of Spastics, Inc., Edinburgh, 145, *see also*
Credits; Society for the Aid of Thalidomide Children, Scottish Branch,
12, 13; Women's Voluntary Service
Housing Association, Bromley, England, xii, 169, *see also* Credits
Grippers, 80
"Growth" clothing, 110

Hague Rehabilitation Center, The, 24,
145, 154, 167. *See also* Credits
Hamilton, Ann, 48
"Handicabs," 185, 186
Handicrafts, 130, 139, 196
Hand limitations, tools and devices for
those with, 23, 24, 29–32, 39–44,
49, 50, 113–117, 129–142, 144
Hands, use of both, 22, 26, 28, 34. *See
also* Work simplification
Head covering, for infants, 53
Heart Association of Maryland, 27. *See
also* Credits
Hemlines, 116–117
High chairs, 38
Hobbies, 130, 195, 196. *See also* Gar-
dening
Holding: avoidance of, 26; mechanical
devices for, 28, 126, 130, 134. *See
also* Work simplification
Holland. *See* The Netherlands
Home bound, 186, 187
Home care, 186
Home Economics Extension Service: 103,

136, 171, 174. *See also* Credits
Homemaker Health-Aide Services, 186
Homemakers, number of: 3, 8
Homemaking skills: for children, 9, 10–
13, 55; for men and women, 1, 3, 4,
6–9, 14–17, 37, 38
Home management: 1–4, 9, 19–28, 123;
adaptation of equipment in, 25;
cleaning as part of, 137; dishwashing as part of, 20; economic value
of, 3; by the elderly, 6–9; family
cooperation in, 19, 37; housekeeping
standards for, 19–21; food preparation as part of, xii, 4, 5, 14, 16, 24;
independence in, xii, 1, 17, 24; laundry practices in, 21, 29–32, 138; by
men, 1, 14, 16, 38; tasks involved
in, 1. *See also* Work simplification;
Household equipment and devices;
Clothing selection and adaptation
Hooks and eyes, 80
Horseback riding, 183, 192: stirrups for
amputee engaged in, 183
Hospitals: 14, 17, 186. *See also* Rehabilitation centers and Hospitals
Household equipment and devices, 19,
21, 24, 25, 29, 39, 45, 50, 51, 123–
149: adaptation of, 207, 208; for
child care, 33–36, 39–41, 45–51,
145; for cleaning, 6, 27, 137, 157,
158; for dishwashing, 20, 128, 135,
144, 157, 162; multiple use of, 25;
for extending reach, 141; for food
preparation, xii, 24, 28, 33–36, 55,
124, 126, 127, 129–133, 157, 160,
161, 163, 169, 170–174; for opening
bottles and cans, 15, 134, 141; for
doing laundry, 21, 29–32, 138, 141;
selection of, 19, 24, 29, 39, 41, 50,
51, 60, 123–152, 157, 158, 160–
165; for sewing and mending, 139,
140; for sinks, adaptation of standard type, 11, 33, 47, 128, 207, 208;
sources of, 217–219; for stabilizing
and holding, 11, 15, 27, 28, 31, 124,
125, 126, 128, 129, 134, 136, 138,
158, 172; storage of, 33, 141, 156,
160–164, 167, 169, 173, 174; for
stoves, ovens, hotplates, xii, 5, 6,
14, 16, 24, 128, 136, 157, 161, 169,
170, 171. *See also* Trays; Carts;
Chairs; Sinks

Housing: adapted to suit disability, 156–159; designed for persons confined to a wheel chair, 156, 157; for persons with problems of balance, bending and lifting, 158, 159; apartment, 175; "barrier free," 154, 155–159, 168, 169; church sponsored, 175; condominium, 175; cooperative, 177; family home, 8; for elderly, 153, 175; for handicapped, 154–174; fraternal organization sponsorship of, 175; "Functional Home for Easier Living," 155; grandparent's apartment, 175; "health houses," 154; to suit disabilities, 155–159, 168, 169; invalid flats, 154; legislation in field of, 154; mobile homes, 176; municipal, 175; recreational vehicles as, 185; retirement communities, 175, 176; security of, 175, 176; segregated, 153; trailers, 176; trends in Europe and United States, 153, 154; for veterans, 154, 175; villages for handicapped, 177. See also Kitchens; Furniture; Architectural barriers

Hydraulic lift, 151, 184

I.C.T.A. Information Service, Bromma, Sweden, 154. See also Bibliography

Illinois, University of: School of Home Economics, 160, 161; Small Homes Council, 154

Illustrations. See Photographs

Incontinence. See Protective garments

Independence, 1, 6–9, 14, 39, 153, 175, 184; in dressing, 54, 78–80, 91–122; early, for children, 54–57, 62–72; in housing, 7–9, 175–180, 185; for adults in performing household tasks, xii, 1–7, 14–17, 163, 166; for children, 9–13, 55; in transportation, 153. See also Housing

India: All-India Institute of Medical Science Department of Social Work, New Delhi, 170; Journal of Rehabilitation in Asia, Appendix H; Tyagi, S. L., United States Educational Foundation in India, 152; Y.W.C.A., Madras, 170. See also Credits

Industrial engineers, 18, 19, 22

Infants, care of: adaptation of equipment in, 33, 40–42, 45–49, 51, 51, 206; bathing equipment for, 4, 40–50; bottles and nipples for, 49; clothing for, 52, 53; clothing storage for, 39, 40; use of cribs, 40, 41, 45, 203; use of dressing cart, 25; use of dressing table, 25, 45; adaptation of equipment to suit disability, 25, 38, 40–45, 201–206; equipment for multiple use in, 25; use of feeding tables and high chairs, 49, 50; formula preparation in, 33–36, 49; foot rests for infant chair, 50; use of plastic seats for carrying, 50; use of play pens, 38, 51; safety precautions in, 44, 47, 48, 50; selection of equipment for, 39; use of trays for infant chair, 50, 51; toileting equipment for, 50; arrangement of work centers for bathing and dressing, 40–46

International Symbol of Access, 179

Institutional care, 1, 7, 8, 9, 17. See also Independence

Institute of British Architects, 154

Institute of Rehabilitation Medicine, New York University Medical Center, 15, 16, 91, 92, 100, 101, 155, 172. See also Credits (Former Name: Institute of Physical Medicine and Rehabilitation)

Invalid Foundation Orthopedic Hospital, Helsinki, 126, 127, 133. See also Credits

Ironing: equipment for, 23, 138, 139; family cooperation in, 21, 23; how to limit, 19, 32, 88–90; with hand limitations, 138

Insurance for homemakers, 154

Jackets and capes, children's, 117; women's, 92, 99

Judson, Julia S., Preface

Kenny Rehabilitation Institute, 137

Kimonos, infants, 53

Kitchens: adaptations to suit physical limitations, xii, 3, 4–6, 10–16, 20, 24, 33, 124, 126–136, 141–143, 148–149, 156–163, 166–169, 171–174, 207; sinks for, see Sinks; research in

Protective pants, 85; for infants, 53, 85
Puppets, 72
Purpose of life, 7, 196

"Questioning Approach," 19–21, 41. *See also* Work simplification

Range of motion, 22, 23
Ramps, xii, 2, 56, 153, 156, 179, 168, 184. *See also* Architectural barriers
Raymond Poincare Hospital, Garches, France, 128, 131, 166
Reach, devices for extension of, 141. *See also* Storage
Recreation: archery, 191, art, 65–67; baseball, 2; barrier-free design for, 179, 180; basketball, 190; bowling, 190, 192; cooking, 55; dramatics, 70, 72; fishing, 180; gardening, xii, 76, 193; handicrafts, 140; hobbies, 194, 195; javelin throwing, 191; music, 64; nature study, 74–77, 180; reading, to children, 58, 63, 188; riding, 183, 192; ski touring, 181; skiing, one track, 181, 182; snowmobiling, 181, 182; storytelling, 68–78; swimming, 180; trails, 180, 183; travel, *see* Transportation and Travel. *See also* Play Activities
Recreational vehicles, 185
Rehabilitation: bus designed for teaching, 136; services, 2, 3, 186, 199. *See also* Vocational rehabilitation
Rehabilitation Centers and Hospitals: All India Institute of Medical Services, New Delhi, 170; Australian Red Cross, 126; Fitzsimmons Veterans Hospital, Denver, *see* Woolverton, Mary, 183; The Hague, Netherlands, 24, 145, 154, 167, 172; Institute of Rehabilitation Medicine, New York City, 15, 16, 91, 92, 100, 101, 155, 172; Invalid Foundation Orthopedic Hospital and School, Helsinki, 126, 127, 133; Kings College Hospital, London, 168; Kenny Rehabilitation Institute, 137; Kivela Hospital, Helsinki, 140; Ohio Goodwill Industries, Cincinnati, 142, 149, 173; Orange County General Hospital, California,

7, 27, 131; Orthopedic Hospital, Copenhagen, 11, 125, 135, 139; Princess Margaret Rose Hospital, Edinburgh, 12, 13; Public Health Restoration Center, Saskatchewan, Canada, 4, 6, 124, 131, 132, 145; Raymond Poincare Hospital, Garches, France, 131, 166; Rehabilitation Institute of Chicago, 10, 131; Rehabilitation Institute of Greater Detroit, 137; Royal Devonshire Hospital, Buxton, England, 168; School and Hospital for Crippled Children, Sioux Falls, South Dakota, 11; University of Michigan Medical Center, 3, 124; University of Cincinnati Medical Center, *see* Bibliography; Veterans Administration Hospital, East Orange, New Jersey, 6, 187; Veterans Administration Hospital, Tucson, Arizona, *see* Hohmann, G. H., Bibliography; Vocational Guidance and Rehabilitation Services, Cleveland, 96, 97; Walter Reed Army Medical Center, 14. *See also* Bibliography and credits
Rehabilitation Institute of Chicago: 10, 131. *See also* Credits
Rehabilitation Institute of Greater Detroit, 137. *See also* Credits
Rehabilitation Services Administration, 189
Reinforcements: belt loops, 114; braces, 100, 112; for elbows and knees, 88, 100; seam, 86, 87, 112; sleeve, 87, 112; socks and stockings, 118; underwear, 120
Research Related to the Handicapped and the Elderly: American Heart Association (kitchens), 171; Colorado State University, Department of Occupational Therapy (kitchen planning, food preparation, work simplification), 5; Connecticut Easter Seal Society (clothing for handicapped children), 230; University of Cincinnati Medical Center (sex adjustments), *see* Bibliography; University of Connecticut, School of Home Economics (clothing for handicapped children, 230; self help clothing for children, 103–122;

liography; housing for, 1, 175–177; and housekeeping skills, 6, 14–17; institution residents, 17; prosthetic aid for, 14; and sports, 181–183, 190, 191; and war casualties, 14–17

Veterans Administration Hospital, East Orange, New Jersey, 6, 187. *See also* Credits

Vista, 189

Visiting Nurse Association, 186

Vocational Guidance and Rehabilitation Services, Cleveland, 96, 97

Vocational Rehabilitation, 2, 3, v, 186

Volunteer and paid employment, 187–189. *See also* ACTION

Waistbands, adjustable, 10, 97, 100, 110

Walker, Mrs. Margaret Harvey, 144. *See also* Credits

Wall, Jessie S., *see* Preface

Walter Reed Army Medical Center, 14. *See also* Credits

War casualties, 14–17

Water play, 57

Wheelchairs: barrier-free homes and, xii, 155–159; battery-powered, 147, 168; clothing adjustments for users of, 92, 101, 102, 112, 113; devices for lifting into car trunk, 146, 209, 210; foot-powered, 149; for narrow spaces, 148; gasoline-powered outdoor, 150; hydraulic, 148; kitchens adapted to users of, 157; narrow indoor, 148; storage in car trunk, 146; trailers for, 147; transfer to car from, 148; trays for, 14, 36, 143, 145. *See also* Work simplification and Transportation and travel

Wheelchair trailers, 147

Whitaker, Alice P., *see* Preface

Widowed, distribution by age, 8; living arrangements for, 8

Women, clothing for, 78–98

Women's Voulntary Services, Housing Association, xii, 169. *See also* Credits

Woolverton, Mary, photographer, 83

Work centers. *See* Work simplification

Work methods, 19

Working heights. *See* Work simplification

Work simplification: 1, 2, 9, 19–46, 123–175: adaptation of equipment for, 00; in child care, 25, 37–53; in cleaning, 27, 237, 157, 158; and placing controls within easy reach, 24, 29, 30, 39, 42, 156–158, 162, 165, 167–169, 171; and design of interiors, 185; for dishwashing, 20, 28, 135; and ease in transporting, 21, 25–27, 29, 30, 32, 36, 39, 41, 45, 46, 57, 137, 143, 145–147, 201; and easy flow of work, 23, 29, 40, 45; and efficient use of the body, 26; and family cooperation, 2, 19, 21, 23, 29, 37, 87; and formula making, 33–36; and food preparation, xii, 5, 24, 27, 124–127, 129–132; and holding, avoidance of, 26; mechanical devices for, 26, 28, 31, 126, 128, 130, 134, 137, 138, 140, 141; laundry practices for, 21, 23, 28, 30–32, 138, 141; principles involved in, 19–28; the questioning approach to, 19–21, 41; range of motion in, 22–24; sitting to work for, 26, 27, 45–53; selection of tools and equipment for, 24, 25, 27, 29, 33, 39, 41; sliding things instead of lifting for, 24, 26, 27; storage of supplies and equipment for, 22, 23; using other parts of the body for, 27, 31, 32, 42, 43, 134, 138; use of both hands for, 22, 26, 28, 34; use of lowest class motions for, 26, 27; use of gravity and momentum for, 26, 28, 32, 46, 158; work centers for, 5, 22, 23, 39–46; working heights for, xii, 11, 16, 21–24, 31–33, 36, 39, 45, 46, 126, 127, 135, 141, 156, 174, 179. *See also* Home Management; Storage; Adaptation of Equipment

World Magazine, 9

Wrinkle-resistant fabrics, 86, 89, 90

Zimmerman, Muriel E., 91

Zippers, 79, 94, 98, 100, 101, 117

Zmola, Gertrude M., *see* Preface